G. F. Watts

A Nineteenth Century Phenomenon

Chosen by
JOHN GAGE

Introduction by
CHRIS MULLEN

The Whitechapel Art Gallery
High Street, London E1

22nd January
to 3rd March
1974

ACKNOWLEDGEMENTS

The policy of The Whitechapel Art Gallery for the past two years has been to return the Gallery to the people who live nearby. This exhibition of G. F. Watts is a part of that policy. Watts was a good friend of Canon Barnett, founder of this Gallery, and before The Whitechapel Art Gallery was built showed many of his paintings in the old School House – where Barnett held immensely popular exhibitions. It was these 'picture shows' in the School House which inspired Barnett to raise the money to build The Whitechapel Art Gallery.

The Gallery has been able to mount the Watts exhibition by making use of part of a farewell present from Lord Bearsted, Chairman of the Board of Trustees of The Whitechapel Art Gallery from 1949 until earlier this year. The present Chairman of the Board, Mr. Pat Matthews, and the Trustees are grateful to Lord Bearsted for having given so generously of his services during those glorious albeit sometimes difficult years. The other part of Lord Bearsted's gift is to be spent on the exhibition 'Paintings of The City of London' to be held next February.

Of special pleasure to those concerned with organising the present exhibition has been the kind co-operation of all the lenders. An exhibition like this is entirely dependent on loaned pictures. Wilfrid Blunt, Curator of the Watts Gallery at Compton, and his assistant Richard Jefferies, have been most generous with their time and expertise. The Director and Trustees of The Tate Gallery have overstepped the bounds of duty by lending the centrepiece of this exhibition *A Story from Boccaccio* which has been restored in record time by A. W. Lucas. The Whitechapel Art Gallery would also like to thank the following for their assistance: The Arts Council, The Witt Library, The Treasurer and Masters of the Bench of Lincoln's Inn, Jeremy Maas and Oriole Mullen.

The Whitechapel Art Gallery has been fortunate, too, to have had the help of a grand supporting staff – both paid and voluntary – as well as a multitude of kind friends.

LENDERS

Her Majesty Queen Elizabeth II
Aberdeen Art Gallery
County Borough of Bournemouth Art Gallery and
    Museums
Bristol City Art Gallery
Cambridge, Fitzwilliam Museum
Carlisle Art Gallery
The Rt. Hon. The Earl of Clarendon
Compton, The Trustees of the Watts Gallery
The Farringdon Collection Trust
Brinsley Ford, Esq.
Mrs. Charlotte Frank
Leicester Museum and Art Gallery
London, Guildhall Art Gallery

London, The Royal Borough of Kensington and Chelsea
London, The Cricket Memorial Gallery
    Marylebone Cricket Club
London, Trustees of the National Portrait Gallery
London, Trustees of the Tate Gallery
London, Victoria & Albert Museum
City of Norwich Museums
Oxford, The Visitors of the Ashmolean Museum
Paris, Musée du Louvre
Port Sunlight, Trustees of the Lady Lever Art Gallery
Kerrison Preston, Esq.
Thomas Stainton, Esq.
York City Art Gallery

From the collection of the Royal Photographic Society

'The Whisper of the Muse', photograph of G. F. Watts by Julia Cameron c. 1865

FOREWORD

G. F. Watts: a Nineteenth Century Phenomenon

'Ah, Watts. Yes. His literature was bad', said Yeats, setting the painter in a company where he could scarcely shine against the brilliance of the novelists, whose own feeling for scale and significance and universal themes has lasted better. But we have seen enough Symbolist art in recent years in London – Rodin, Böcklin, Moreau – to feel less dismissive about literary painting, and Watts at least came to write his own inventive *libretti*. The art he cherished, and not simply the portraits he painted 'in order to purchase the luxury of bestowing', deserves another look.

To his contemporaries Watts seemed aloof, a private man, drawn away from their preoccupations by that striving upwards ('Up the hillside of Excellence ... the way if not always rugged is always steep') which is such a recurrent image with him. They were wrong. He was a painter of his century, touched by the urgency of each new aesthetic impulse. The range of styles and subjects in this exhibition is witness enough to that.

And not only in art. Those paradoxes of thought and feeling that muddy our understanding of that monstrous century are also those at the heart of Watts' personality. A chilling aside like 'I live in habitual consciousness of larger issues, and cannot long be affected by anything of purely personal interest', is belied by the searching tenderness of many drawings, and by the recurrent informal portraits of women and girls. The academic dismissal of all but the figure as a painterly language runs counter to the evident involvement in landscape; to Watts' insight, rare in its time, that the Greeks showed a supreme sensitivity to landscape, too. Watts was open to feelings he could not manage. Politics (like love) must be kept at bay, 'not because I do not care, but because I cannot trust myself not to become absorbed by them'. But politics provoked that ravaged, Goya-like head in *Under a Dry Arch*, as love brought about his most affectionate portraits, *Choosing* and *Lady Holland on a Day Bed*. We must be grateful for such fleeting commitments, even when they threw up embarrassments like the essay on the Boer War (*Our Race as Pioneers*) and the many flaccid or mawkish Allegories of Love.

It is not as if Watts were the apologist of Great Victorianism, as Lytton Strachey might have us believe. The high-mindedness, the cult of Beauty, is flawed by pessimism, and a violence in paint that exploits Tintoretto more than the serene Italian Primitives Watts so often invokes. His chauvinism is shot through by despair at the ugly futility of an Empire based on Mammon.

The easy banality of his early language, for example in *Life's Illusions* (Tate Gallery), gives place in *Hope* and *The Sower of the Systems*, to images that still have power. With its obsessive attention to Italian Renaissance models, Watts' art embodies in its way that hopeless yearning of the northerner for the South that we recognise in Ibsen and in Munch.

'The birthplace and natural dwelling-place of art' [he wrote] 'must be in a land of sun and leisure, but we must tempt it at least to be with us if only as a guest. As far as colour is concerned, there can be no great art that has not for its religious basis sun-worship. It is by the sun's influence that we live and breathe and have activity, in fact life!'

The comedy of Watts' life often flows from discrepancies in scale. In the mid-1880's, G. F. Watts, R.A., Honorary Doctor of Canon Law at Oxford, 'the foremost painter of the nude in England' (*Pall Mall Gazette*), and 'broadly speaking, the greatest of our Royal Academicians' (*The Times*), presented Lords Cricket Ground not with an allegorical mural exhorting to Play the Game, but with a series of lively studies of early batsmen. The inveterate punster of the English fireside, the after-dinner soloist of *Tom Bowling* and *Sally in our Alley*, when he ventured to monumentalise such sensibilities, in *Tasting the First Oyster*, or *When Poverty comes in at the Door, Love flies out at the Window*, fell flat on his face. There is something touchingly inappropriate in his adoption of the *persona*, as well as the style of Titian (the skull-cap and the neat beard come straight from Titian's Uffizi self-portrait): this frail, withdrawn idealist, distrustful of honours and contemptuous of money, in the guise of one of the most robust, extrovert and grasping of Renaissance artists, always ready for the main chance.

And yet when Mrs. Russell Barrington, in the catalogue of the New York Watts exhibition of 1884-5, described his approach to painting exclusively in terms of Titian, she put her finger on an aspect of his work that sites him firmly in his own times: the reluctance to call a halt. Like Titian (and like Turner and Moreau), Watts began far more paintings than he could ever complete, and worked them over many years. Like Rodin's, many of his later compositions were elements in a vast scheme of philosophical art that he could never bring together. The shelter of patronage from Holland House and a steady income from portraiture freed Watts for that indulgence in technical experiment, associated in England since Reynolds with the chimera of the Venetian Secret, and that involvement with the impossible that characterise so much of the art of the nineteenth and twentieth centuries.

'The qualities I aim at are too abstract to be attained' – Watts wrote to Ruskin – 'or perhaps to produce any effect, if attained. My instincts cause me to strive after things that are hardly within the province of art'.

In a moment of despair, he signed a work *G. F. Watts Finis*: he had lost the will to go on. Ruskin came in and added in chalk, *et initium*. It was his most perceptive criticism, and this constant openness to revision is what makes Watts' artistic personality so sympathetic to us.   JOHN GAGE

CHRONOLOGY

1817 Born in London on 23 February. As a child, suffered from ill-health and did not go to school. Learned to read at home – from the Bible, a translation of Homer, Scott and Jane Austen. From the age of ten, frequented the studio of William Behnes, the sculptor, who introduced him to the Elgin Marbles.

1835 Admitted to R.A. schools but attended regularly for only a very short time.

1837 First exhibits at the R.A. – *The Wounded Heron* and *Miss Hopkins*. Met his first important patron, Constantine Ionides; eventually painted portraits of five generations of the Ionides family.

1843 Awarded a first prize of £300 for his cartoon *Caractacus* in the first Houses of Parliament competition.

1843-7 Left for Italy. After six weeks in Paris, went on to Florence, where he became the guest of Lord and Lady Holland; first at the Casa Feroni, later at the Villa Medicea at Careggi, just outside the city. Accompanied the Hollands on visits to Rome, Naples, etc. When the Hollands left Florence late in 1845, Watts stayed on at Careggi with Lady Duff Gordon and her daughters. Entered the 1847 Houses of Parliament competition and returned to England with his entry, *Alfred inciting the Saxons*, which won a first prize of £500.

1848 Painted *Time and Oblivion*, first of the big allegorical pictures. Met Ruskin.

1849-50 Studio at 30 Charles Street, Berkeley Square. Painted *The Irish Famine*.

1850 Visited Ireland, as guest of Aubrey de Vere, the poet, and his family.

1851 Became the permanent guest of Mr. and Mrs. Thoby Prinsep at old Little Holland House (Mrs. Prinsep: 'He came to stay three days, he stayed thirty years', an exaggeration, but true in substance). Little Holland House, the seat of a semi-Bohemian salon, thronged with celebrities: Tennyson, Thackeray, Gladstone, Joachim, Herschel, Pre-Raphaelites, etc. – also Mrs. Prinsep's numerous sisters; among them Julia Margaret Cameron and the beautiful Countess Somers. Large studios added to the house for Watts' benefit.

1852 Offered to decorate Euston Station with frescoes, without remuneration except for the cost of scaffolding and pigments. The proposal rejected by the Directors of the London and North-Western Railway.

1853 Short visit to Italy – Genoa, Florence, Padua, Venice, etc.

1855-6 Spent several months in Paris, accompanied by Arthur Prinsep; studio at 10 Rue des Saints Pères. Painted *Princess Lieven*.

1859 The fresco *The School of Lawgivers* in the New Hall of Lincoln's Inn, begun in 1853, completed.

1863 Gave evidence before the Royal Commission appointed to inquire into the position of the Royal Academy.

1864 Married Ellen Terry (aged sixteen); they separated the following year.

1865 Met Charles Hilditch Rickards, a Manchester business man who became his greatest patron. At the time of his death in 1887 Rickards owned about sixty pictures by Watts.

1867 Elected A.R.A. and R.A. in the same year. Became seriously interested in sculpture; new sculpture studio constructed in the garden of Little Holland House.

1870 Began the equestrian statue *Hugh Lupus* (finished in 1883) for the then Marquis of Westminster; also first studies for *Physical Energy*.

1875 Little Holland House demolished. Watts lived at The Briary, Freshwater, Isle of Wight, where the Prinseps had moved the previous year. He had the house built for them when it became clear that Little Holland House would have to be given up.

1876 Out of touch with his portrait practice on the Isle of Wight, Watts settled at No. 6 Melbury Road – new 'Little Holland House', near the site of the old building. Without the Prinseps and their relatives, led quieter life. Continued to spend winters at The Briary.

1879 Wrote the article 'The Present Conditions of Art' for the *Nineteenth Century* (published February 1880).

1880 First one-man exhibition, of pictures belonging to Rickards, at the Manchester Institution.

1881-2 First London one-man exhibition at the Grosvenor Gallery. Began to be famous for his allegorical pictures; hitherto had been known mainly as a portraitist.

1884-5 One-man exhibition at the Metropolitan Museum, New York.

1885 Offered baronetcy by Gladstone – declined.

1886-7 Married Mary Fraser-Tytler and went on trip to Malta, Egypt, Athens and Constantinople. On return, friction between the new Mrs. Watts and Mrs. Russell Barrington, an old friend, pupil, neighbour and future biographer of the painter. An arrangement eventually made whereby Mrs. Barrington's visits occurred only in Mrs. Watts' absence.

1887-8 Winter and spring in Malta, Naples, Mentone and Aix-les-Bains.

1890 Visited Isle of Wight to paint Tennyson's portrait; last meeting of the two old friends.

1891 Occupied new winter home at Limnerslease, Compton, Surrey.

1894 Second offer of baronetcy by Gladstone – again declined.

1898 Visit to the Scottish Highlands. Began work (at the age of eighty-one) on a colossal statue of Tennyson, now at Lincoln.

1902 Accepted the newly instituted Order of Merit.

1903 Finished the Tennyson statue, but did not live to see it cast.

1904 Last revisions of *Physical Energy*. Early in June, taken ill with a sore throat. Died, London, 1 July.

G. F. Watts: The House of Life

The painter William Rothenstein, who had visited G. F. Watts and who had helped Canon Barnett to run exhibitions at Whitechapel, wrote in 1931, 'Our high estimate of Watts and his paintings I still feel to be justified ... His construction is often faulty and his subjects are admittedly didactic; yet he is likely to take his place finally as one of the most richly endowed artists of the English school. Today the epic spirit is under a cloud, because it does not now come naturally to modern painters. But to Watts it did come naturally, and the mention of his name evokes a luminous world of his own creation. This is in itself a proof of his genius'.

Everybody agreed – there was no-one like G. F. Watts. He stood apart, not really belonging to the age. While other artists of the late nineteenth century could stride the grousemoors, play the stock market and sail their yachts, Watts allowed himself no respite from work, getting up at five, perhaps playing his violin until the light broke, then settling down to paint until dusk, stabbing and crushing the crumbling paint into the pitted surfaces that had sometimes been thirty years in the making. Images would appear and disappear in the play of the paint, before the canvas returned to the heaps on the studio floor. Perhaps a friend would come in and play the piano as he worked and listen as Watts expounded the moral theme of the painting then on the easel. As the evening drew in he would pack up for the day, and after a light meal would relax on a couch while his wife or some adoring visitor read to him. When, on Sundays, other artists would throw open their studios to show works to prospective customers, Watts would show himself surrounded by his paintings, an Oracle for the idle rich and the industrious poor alike. His paintings were addressed to both. They were destined in Watts' own mind not for the drawing-rooms of the well-to-do, but for some large building in which they could hang as a series, which he always referred to as *The House of Life*.

Watts was born in 1817. His parents were poor and as a child he suffered from ill-health. Largely self taught, he was active as a portrait painter, until at the age of 26, in 1843, he entered a competition run by the Government to discover likely mural painters to decorate the New Palace of Westminster. To his great surprise, his cartoon of *Caractacus* won a £300 prize. With the money he went to Italy, for that obligatory consultation with the Ancients and the Old Masters. The years 1843-7 were the watershed in his career. During this time he made many powerful friends, notably Lord and Lady Holland, he made his first experiments in fresco painting, and was exposed to the art of the Italian Renaissance.

When he returned to England in 1847, and won another prize in this series of competitions, and when he was commissioned to begin painting in true fresco at Westminster, it is no wonder that G. F. Watts began to have greater ambitions. In the 1850's he made a name for himself as an authority on mural painting and particularly on working in true fresco. In 1852 he offered to paint *The Progress of Cosmos* for the vast spaces of the Great Hall of Euston Station. He painted murals in three private houses, and during the decade an enormous mural, *The School of Law-Givers,* on one wall of the Hall at Lincoln's Inn, London.

In the 1860's Watts was involved in the decoration of St. Paul's Cathedral and the South Kensington Museum, but before he committed himself to anything more ambitious, he suddenly began to lose interest in mural painting, the passion of his youth. Before the 1860's he had even produced easel paintings in the manner of fresco, rather flat and dull, using large simple masses. During the 1860's, he experimented with various pigments and grounds to get a rougher surface.

Instead of thinking out the balance of great sweeps of form and colour from preparatory drawings, Watts became far more interested in the accidental, in the inspirational. In the late 1860's he was continuing to explore the grand abstractions of his youth, in new configurations, and for the first time, in sculpture. During most of his working life Watts was known chiefly for his portraits, but in the 1880's his allegorical works were finally recognised, bringing him fame. Thus began the Cult of Watts, expressed in interviews with the Great Man, in widely distributed reproductions of his paintings and countless monographs on his work. Such was the impact of this Cult that Roger Fry complained on Watts' death in 1904 that, 'Mr. Watts was lavish both in painting pictures and in presenting them to the public, so that his departure is the departure of a personality too familiar for impartial admiration'. Watts was compared with Whistler 'whose genius was always surrounded with a certain glamour of remoteness'.

Now that recent exhibitions of Whistler's work have reversed this judgement it is likely that Watts' work will be received with more sympathy and understanding than it was in 1904. His reputation did survive, and better than Leighton's or Burne-Jones'. People like Sydney Colvin, Frank Brangwyn and Walter Sickert saw Watts as a painter uniquely qualified to work on a large scale.

Accounts of Watts in 1848, the year of Revolution in Europe, reveal the conflicts in his character and his art. He was in bad health, very depressed, unsure and close to some nervous collapse. His paintings show two distinctive tendencies, towards Realism, and towards Allegory.

Such was the immediacy of the impact that social and political events of 1848 had on Watts, that he could not remove them into allegory and myth. *The Irish Famine* of 1850, one of four realistic pictures depicting the sorrows and suffering of the poor, registered the artist's specific observations when, on a visit to Ireland, he witnessed the failure of the potato crop. *Found Drowned* of 1848-50 is again a response to an event he himself witnessed. In *Under a Dry Arch* and *The Song of the Shirt,* he concentrated on the helpless suffering of women. Watts was never to return to Social Realism – his later Mystical Imperialism was veiled in misty allegory – but he managed to convert his concern for Society into the encouragement of contacts with the poor and unfortunate of London.

He supported efforts to get an art gallery for South London. He lent pictures to exhibitions at Whitechapel organised by Canon Barnett. In 1888, for instance, he lent 10 pictures for the winter, 'They warm hearts by their colour, and suggest thoughts which cannot be put into words . . . men and women who turn away from preachers and from books stop before the pictures which tell of Life and Death' wrote Canon Barnett. Parties of people from the East End came out to Watts' house at 6, Melbury Road, Kensington. A friend remembered that one afternoon 'crowded together were a number of poor people, living habitually with nothing but the most squalid ugliness in their surroundings, looking with eager eyes at the visions of his creation, and listening most earnestly to the explanations of the ideas and meanings in them'. It is significant that when Watts came to use art as monument in his later years, he did so, not with a mythological theme, like that he had chosen for the proposed Euston mural, the *Progress of Cosmos,* but with Postman's Park in St. Botolph's, Aldersgate, London, a sort of *Campo Santo* to commemorate the heroic deeds of the common people, each deed recorded on a plaque.

In addition, Watts supported the Kyrle Society, organised in 1877 by Miranda Hill to bring 'beauty home to the people' by decorating working men's clubs, meeting places, hospitals, schools and mission rooms. As well as lending pictures and providing hospitality, he also helped organise concerts in the East End. Another movement he supported was the drive to clear more spaces open for recreation. As an extension of this work, he also encouraged Gertie Tippla's Anti-Tight-Lacing Society, which attacked 'waywardness of female fashion'.

To return to 1848, the other distinctive tendency in Watts' art was towards Allegory. He constantly cautioned himself in high moral tones against the temptations of Life. *Life's Illusions* of 1849 shows a knight on horseback – the usual way Watts introduced his own presence into a picture – in pursuit of a bubble and oblivious of the precipice at his horse's hoofs. A soaring group of naked women, and the trappings of power, warn against the lures of seduction and vainglory. The *Fata Morgana* of 1848 makes the theme of sexual frustration more explicit, in the piquant contrast of opulent flesh and glinting armour.

The most important allegorical scheme Watts devised was *The House of Life.* Watts had visited the Sistine Chapel in Rome to see Michelangelo's frescoes in 1845. 'His *cicerone* told him he knew he would be disappointed, for the light was never good enough to see the work, but at last his eagerness prevailed, and they stepped under that matchless roof to find the whole chapel flooded with light . . . George Watts, prepared as he was, was nevertheless unexpectedly overwhelmed.' The impact of this mystical revelation inspired him to commit himself to paint for the cost of his materials alone a series of frescoes in a hall of great size, to illustrate the history of mankind. This he called *The House of Life.* 'The ceiling to be covered with the uniform blue of space, on which should be painted the Sun, the Earth and the Moon, as it is by their several revolutions and dependence upon each other that we have a distinct notion of, and

are able to measure and estimate, the magnitude of Time. The progress of Time, and its consequent effect, I would illustrate for the purpose of conveying a moral lesson – the design of Time and Oblivion would be exactly in its place. To complete the design, the Earth should be attended by two figures symbolic of the antagonistic forces, Attraction and Repulsion. I would then give, perhaps upon one half of the ceiling, which might be divided with a gold band on which the zodiac might be painted, a nearer view of earth, and by a number of gigantic figures stretched out at full length represent a range of mountains typifying the rocky structure or skeleton. These I would make very grand and impressive, in order to emphasise the insignificance of man. The most important (to us) of the constellations should shine out of the deep ultramarine firmament. Silence and Mighty Repose should be stamped upon the character and disposition of the giants; and the revolving centuries and cycles should glide, personified by female figures of great beauty, beneath the crags upon which the mighty forms should lie, to indicate (as compared with the effect upon man and his works) the non-effect of time upon them. . . . Then I would begin with man himself, trace him through his moral and political life; first the hunter stage, gaining, through the medium of his glimmering yet superior intelligence, advantages over the stronger yet inferior animals, almost his equals. Next the pastoral state, his intelligence further developed to the consequent improvement of his condition: serviceable animals domesticated, reclaimed by his thoughtful care, the stronger and finer subdued by the force of his will, aided by all-conquering intelligence. This is the Golden Age, the age of poetry. Of experience comes tradition, of tradition is born poetry, here performing its natural and legitimate function – instructing. This portion of the work might be rendered most beautifully, since in this period of the history of society it is possible the human animal enjoyed the greatest possible amount of happiness, equally removed from the penalties of ambition, and from the degradation of a precarious and merely animal existence. There would be a great chance of exquisite subjects to illustrate this epoch, and here might be introduced the episode of Job.

'Next should be man – the tyrant – the insidious oppressor – the slave, a dweller in cities – the Egyptians raise the pyramids – their mythology – the habits of the people.' This extraordinary programme was to end with a pageant of the progress of civilisation through Palestine, Assyria, Persia, India, Greece and Rome, each with its mythology and representative men. It would trace the dawning of the Christian era; the fall of Jerusalem; the rise of Saracen power and the preaching of Peter the Hermit. Watts was never to start painting this in fresco. But the idea inspired many oil paintings. The programme was always changing. Watts later included the *Eve* series and the *Cain* series, *The Court of Death, Chaos, Physical Energy* and *Time, Death and Judgement.* By 1896, the original grandiose scheme had shrunk to a hope that eventually these paintings might, like Munch's *Frieze of Life* of 1892, be assembled together in a public place.

It is difficult here in the restricted space of the Whitechapel Art Gallery to do justice to Watts' flair for the monumental. *The Court of Death,* the definitive version, measures 167″ × 108″, and was proposed as a decoration to a mortuary chapel for London paupers. The casts of *Physical Energy* stare out from Kensington Gardens and from the Cecil Rhodes Memorial near Cape Town. Watts' *Chaos* was a study of those full-length gigantic figures to be painted on the ceiling of the great hall.

But in 1848 Watts' dream was far from being fanciful. In Paris, Paul Chenavard had just begun the commission to decorate the *Pantheon.* Charles Blanc was promoting a revival of painting on a large scale, 'murals for the railway stations, frescoes for the temples and palaces of the new Republic'.

During the 1850's the Westminster frescoes had turned into a huge and highly expensive joke. One artist working there summed up the despair, 'I feel how much has been wasted in, as it were, writing in the sand. Time's effacing finger had begun to obliterate at one end while we were painfully working at the other'. Yet during the 1850's Watts was loudly promoting a mural revival and, by implication, his own successes. He wanted murals in town halls, national schools and railway stations. Large reproductions of Flaxman's classical designs could be painted on the walls at Eton, so the boys would 'grow up under the influence of works of beauty of the highest excellence'. Others such as J. R. Herbert believed in the validity of mural painting. The gaols of Britain could be painted with subjects which would impress upon the criminals the importance of a good life. 'Paint your hospitals for the sick with great subjects of miraculous cures from the Gospels. . . . Paint your courts of justice so as to impress witnesses with the abhorrence of falsehood'.

Watts' greatest success was the completion of the Lincoln's Inn fresco, 1853-9, praised immoderately in the press, and by D. G. Rossetti, who found it 'the finest specimen of the method we have seen among modern ones'. Millais called it magnificent. The composition of the figure groups was admired and despite the 'dull, crude and obscure' colours, it was in true fresco, and it appeared to be sticking on the walls. It may not have had those cosmic reflections of *The House of Life,* but it could be construed as 'a progress of civilisation'. It was in a position to influence minds – a reminder to one pillar of society of its awesome heritage.

But, suddenly, just as *The House of Life* was beginning to look a reality, he dropped out of the British Mural revival of the 1860's. He had completed a mural at the Church of St. James the Less, Westminster, and was about to start a lunette in one Court of the South Kensington Museum. Perhaps he came to realise as he was working on the Lincoln's Inn fresco that he could not hope to sustain this single-handed heroic effort. While others used armies of assistants, Watts could never delegate. Perhaps he began to realise the drift in taste in the 1860's away from the didactic towards the decorative. As he looked around him, he saw the men he had anticipated joining him in the vaults of the British Sistine being consulted on the colour schemes of London clubs, allowing their drawings to be amplified into murals by photography, and being paid, like tradesmen, by the square yard for decorative friezes.

Watts just did not have that sureness of touch so vital to the painter in true fresco. One mistake meant cutting out and re-laying the plaster. At a time when he was losing all energy for the task of mural painting, he began to develop the use of rough, granular surface on canvas, using paint from which the oil had been drained out. He made extremely influential experiments using benzine as a vehicle for the pigment. His technique after the 1870's is neatly illustrated by the reaction of a friend who had just visited Leighton's studio. 'That's what I call painting,' she said. 'He covers his brush with paint and makes nice, long, deep, firm strokes.' – 'And what do I do?' asked Watts. 'You paint with everything except the brush . . . with rags, with nasty old bits of paper, and with your thumb.' This inspirational approach to the act of painting brought a welcome spontaneity, and made each version of a subject a fresh statement.

The energy that would have been expended in fresco painting was instead channelled into a prolific output of easel paintings. Some of them were given to provincial museums, and a large number were presented to the National Gallery of British Art.

It is doubtful if any of Watts' schemes would have been realised had it not been for a quality in him that attracted the motherly, and often unmotherly, attentions of dominating and possessive women. We see Watts in Florence needing little persuasion to turn a social call on Lord and Lady Holland into a stay of about two years. In his portraits he saw Lady Holland as a sort of mischievous elder sister with just a hint of the coquette. Watts even painted *Paolo and Francesca* with her features clearly recognisable. In 1845, and alone in the Hollands' villa at Careggi Watts was taken over, virtually with the furniture, by Lady Duff Gordon and her daughters. It is significant that when he came back to England in 1847, no longer in the care of an understanding family, he spent three of the most miserable years of his life until in 1850, lonely and showing all the signs of the permanent invalid, he was taken in by the Prinseps. It was without a shadow of irony that Mrs. Prinsep said, 'He came to stay three days, he stayed thirty years'.

At the Prinseps', Little Holland House, Watts was given the run of his own studio and, at agreed times of the day would appear in his capacity of *Signor,* court painter to a *salon* of beautiful people, intelligent people, and, above all, celebrated people. Apart from the Prinseps, the Pattles and the Somers, the list of those who gathered at Little Holland House was long and distinguished. It included Dickens, Thackeray, Tennyson, Leighton and Millais. The effects of the bad plumbing in the house often allowed Watts to plead ill-health on occasions when he wanted to avoid being lionised. Later in the 1850's we catch a glimpse of Watts through the eyes of William Michael Rossetti. He wrote of Watts, 'His demeanour was thoughtful and sedate and it seemed to be universally understood that he was a man to be approached with respect rather than with anything savouring of the "free and easy" . . .'

For a while in 1864, Watts found himself actually married, to the young Ellen Terry, but as if to deny any suggestion that his anaemic blood was capable of being fired, he maintained that he was doing a social service. Ellen Terry was taken to see Watts in 1862 at the age of 15. He immediately decided to remove her from 'the temptations and abominations of the stage, give her an education and if she continues to have the affection she now feels for me, marry her'. He painted her in *Choosing*, a painting which reveals both a moral approach – she smells a scentless flower – and an appreciation of her beauty.

Watts' courtship consistently followed an altruistic line. When he did marry her, it seemed that he had nothing else to offer. Gossip suggests the marriage was never consummated. Education bored her, she still loved the stage; and she left within the year. They were formally separated in 1865 and divorced in 1877.

Such was Watts' need for security and stability of working conditions, a basic requirement for affection tempered with reserve, that he was content to be passed from hand to hand, like a totem. The similarity increased in the 1880's when Watts became more and more popular with the public, and when he took on the aspect of the Grand Old Man. In 1876, he settled at No. 6, Melbury Road, Kensington, leaving the Prinseps at Freshwater, on the Isle of Wight. For a while he found protection with Mrs. Russell Barrington, his neighbour and future biographer. When she first met him, she was attracted by his handsome face 'with a serious countenance suggesting a latent weariness and melancholy hidden under a crust of reserve'.

But in 1887 he married Mary Fraser-Tytler, a painter and sculptor who had taught at the Whitechapel boys club. She virtually fought Mrs. Barrington off until a mutually acceptable roster of visiting times was devised. From 1891, at Compton, Mary Watts reigned supreme as constant companion and nurse. And it was at Compton that Watts spent his last years until his death in 1904.

Many of the paintings exhibited here at Whitechapel were, in their large versions, meant to be seen together.

This idea can be seen as a European preoccupation; in Gauguin's *Where do we come from? What are we? Where are we going?* (1897), in Rodin's *Gates of Hell,* Jacob Epstein's *Temple of Love* and *Temple of the Sun,* and particularly in Edvard Munch's *Frieze of Life.* Watts' art was particularly meaningful for the Symbolist Movement. They were attracted by his chill sexuality, his anti-materialist stance, and his use of musical analogies. He described *Time and Oblivion* as an 'organ chord swelling and powerful but unmodulated'. He maintained that the forms and colours of the Lincoln's Inn fresco should pervade the building 'like a strain of Handel's music, becoming at one with the architecture'. It is interesting that when W. B. Richmond reviewed the Watts Memorial Exhibition, he wrote, 'One passes from picture to picture without a single jar to one's sense of harmony. Each instrument is in tune, the whole is as a full orchestra that vibrates on one's senses'.

Watts' paintings were widely available on the Continent in reproductions, and in the many exhibitions to which he contributed. Giovanni Costa arranged for Watts to exhibit with the *In Arte Libertas* group in Rome from 1886. In 1893, 22 of his works were shown with the Society of Artists in Munich. In the same year, his *Love and Life* was presented to the Luxembourg Museum.

Perhaps Watts also inspired others by his own example. The German critic Richard Muther described him in 1896 as 'one of those artists who are only to be found in England – an artist who from his youth upwards, has been able to live for his art without regard to profit'. Watts only needed money for the maintenance of house and studios, and for medical expenses. Rather than amass a fortune, as Millais did, Watts tried in the best way he knew to bring comfort and enlightenment to Society.

Although *The House of Life* can never be assembled as Watts intended for the education and inspiration of the People, it is appropriate that it is at Whitechapel in the East End, for which Watts had so much affection and hope, that some reflection of this vision be re-created.

CHRIS MULLEN

CATALOGUE
OIL PAINTINGS

G. F. Watts in his studio at Limnerslease
with 'The Court of Death' 1894

1. Self-Portrait aged 17

Canvas: 22½ × 16 in., 57 × 41 cm.
Coll: Mrs. M. Chapman.
Exb.: Arts Council, 1954-5 (1); Paris, 1972 (318).
Lit.: M.S.W., I, repr. p. 26: Chapman, repr, Pl. 2; Sketchley, pp. 15-16, repr. p. 16.
Lent by the Trustees of the Watts Gallery.
Painted in 1834, the year before he was admitted to the Royal Academy Schools, and three years before he exhibited for the first time. Ten years later, in Florence, Watts was described as a 'most pleasing, open, frank, young man . . . uncommonly handsome, but neither priggish, conceited, pedantic, exquisite or affected'. The sophisticated brushwork evident in this painting suggests a study of Sir Thomas Lawrence's portrait style, e.g. *Portrait of Arthur Atherley* (1792).

2. The Wounded Heron

Canvas: 36 × 28 in., 91 × 71 cm. Signed and dated: *G. F. Watts, 1837.*
Coll.: Bought by Watts from a Newcastle dealer in 1888, after being lost for over fifty years.
Exb.: R.A., 1837 (238); Arts Council, 1954-5 (3); Paris, 1972 (319).
Lit.: Cartwright, p. 4; M.S.W., I, pp. 27-8, repr., III, p. 54; Sketchley, pp. 17, 18; Alston (78), p. 12; Chapman, pp. 17, 147, 172, repr. Pl. 4; Chesterton, pp. 46-7.
Lent by the Trustees of the Watts Gallery.
Watts' first contribution to the Royal Academy exhibitions and painted from a bird bought at a poulterer's shop. It has been suggested that this contains an early expression of that moral element that was so characteristic of Watts' later work. If so, then it seems to have been imposed upon a composition and theme explored by Edwin Landseer, *Hawking in the Olden Time* (Kenwood, Iveagh Bequest) which Watts would have seen at the 1832 RA. Watts also painted *The Shuddering Angel* (Compton, Watts Collection) on the subject of cruelty to birds.

3. Lady Holland

Canvas: 31¾ × 25⅛ in., 81 × 64 cm. Inscr.: *Mary Augusta, Lady Holland, by Watts.*
Coll.: Lady Holland; bequeathed to the Prince of Wales (King Edward VII).
Exb.: R.A., 1848 (307); Arts Council, 1954-5 (6).
Lit.: M.S.W., I, pp. 56, 66; Ilchester, pp. 320-2; Chapman, pp. 24, 149, repr. Pl. 6.
Lent by Her Majesty Queen Elizabeth II.
When Watts arrived in Florence in 1843 he stayed with Lord and Lady Holland at the Casa Feroni, and later at the Villa Medicea, Careggi. This portrait of Mary Augusta (1812-1889), wife of the fourth Lord Holland, was the first picture to be painted at the Casa Feroni. Watts has painted her in a Riviera straw hat. A friend of the Hollands wrote of it as having been painted 'in the style of the *Chapeau de Paille* [by Rubens, National Gallery, London] from some lady having in a joke put one of the country hats on her head . . . it is an extra-ordinary likeness' (Ilchester, p.321).

4. Mountain Landscape

Canvas: 7⅛ × 15¾ in., 18 × 40 cm.
Coll.: Mrs. M. Chapman.
Exb.: Carlisle *Victorian Painters,* 1970 (16).
Lit.: Carlisle catalogue, 1970, p. 10.
Lent by Carlisle Art Gallery.
Painted 1843-47.
See note for *Fiesole* (No. 5)

5. Fiesole

Canvas: 26½ × 34 in., 67 × 86 cm.
Exb.: R.A., 1905 (172).
Lit.: Compton Catalogue, I, p. 55.
Lent by the Trustees of the Watts Gallery.
Painted 1844-5 during Watts' sudden and enthusiastic burst of landscape work, perhaps as a response to the first volume of Ruskin's *Modern Painters,* published in 1843, which encouraged historical painters to study landscape. This work was painted from the hanging gallery under the roof of Lord Holland's villa at Careggi.

6. Lady Holland on a Day Bed

Canvas: 14 × 19 in., 35.5 × 48 cm. Inscribed on back of canvas: *This is to be given to my niece Carrie – M. A. Holland;* also, in the same hand: *Sketch by Watts of Lady Holland, Naples, 1844*
Exb.: Arts Council, 1954-5 (7).
Lit.: Chapman, p. 172, repr. Pl. 7.
Lent by the Trustees of the Watts Gallery.
Lady Holland in a more intimate pose than in her portrait with straw hat (No. 3) but still playing the coquette. Probably painted at the Villa Rocella, Naples, where Watts visited with the Hollands in 1844-5. See Note to No. 3.

7. A Story from Boccaccio

Canvas: 144 × 353½ in., 366 × 898 cm.
Coll.: Presented to the Tate Gallery by the Cosmopolitan Club in 1902.
Exb.: On loan to the Watts Gallery, Compton, during World War II.
Lit.: Barrington, p. 24; M.S.W., I, p. 64; Holman Hunt, *Pre-Raphaelitism and the Pre-Raphaelite Brotherhood*, 1913, I, p. 252.
Lent by the Trustees of the Tate Gallery.
Painted 1844, during the artist's stay in Italy. Watts brought the canvas back to London where it hung beside another painting based on Boccaccio, on the walls of his studio in Charles Street, Berkeley Square. It was still there when the rooms were taken over by the Cosmopolitan Club after 1852. Members of this Club included Watts himself, John Ruskin, Holman Hunt, Henry Layard and Edward Fitzgerald. The painting is here exhibited publicly for the first time in thirty years. Watts illustrates *Philomena's Tale*, the eighth *novella* of the fifth day, from Boccaccio's *Decameron*. Typically Watts has chosen a theme of sexual anxiety. Anastasio degli Onestri of Ravenna persuades the daughter of Paolo Traversaro to marry him by revealing to her a vision of a beautiful naked woman hunted down and devoured by hounds. In keeping with the supernatural elements of the theme, Watts combines Mannerist influences with details of the weird and uncanny derived from Fuseli.

8. Lorenzo de Medici Supported by Two Attendants

Fresco: 17¾ × 13¾ in., 45 × 35 cm.
Lit.: M.S.W., I, p. 63 on the subject.
Lent by the Victoria & Albert Museum.
Having settled as a guest with the Hollands at the Casa Feroni, Florence, Watts made his first attempts at fresco. These works which included a *Flora*, have since disappeared. Two or three years later, at the Villa Medicea where Lorenzo de Medici had died, Watts painted in fresco on the walls of an open loggia the scene when Lorenzo's doctor was drowned in a well for suspected attempts at poisoning. Scenes of famous men on their death-beds, Leonardo, Raphael, etc, were very popular at this time. The work exhibited here relates to that scheme. Probably painted 1845.

9. Paolo and Francesca

Fresco: 24¼ × 18¾ in., 61.5 × 48 cm.
Coll.: Contessa Cottrell.
Exb.: Arts Council, 1954-5 (10).
Lit.: D. Loshak, *Burlington,* 1963, p. 484 and fn. 42.
Lent by the Victoria & Albert Museum.
One of the experiments Watts made in fresco painting while in Italy (see No. 8). The subject, from Dante's *Inferno,* was very popular at this time, with versions by Ingres (1819), C. W. Cope (1837), A. Munro (1851) and J. N. Paton (c.1851), all greatly influenced by Flaxman's outline composition from the *Dante* series. D. Loshak identifies in Francesca the features of Lady Holland, giving to the painting the gloss of sexual guilt. The two lovers were caught and killed by Francesca's outraged husband.

10. Peasants of the Campagna During the Vintage

Canvas: 57 × 66 in., 145 × 168 cm.
Coll.: Purchased from Watts in Florence; The Countess of Clarendon.
Exb.: Grosvenor Gallery, 1881.
Lit.: Compton Catalogue, I, p. 18.
Lent by The Rt. Hon. The Earl of Clarendon.
This idealised study, also known as *The Bulls,* of peasants, painted in 1845, reflects the impact made upon Watts by his first visit to Italy. In 1843 Watts had driven in an open cart from Leghorn to Pisa. 'The vintage was in full beauty and not yet gathered. . . . It was a new world opening before him. As he looked round him he did not wonder that it was from Italy that the highest art had sprung' (Chapman, p. 23). The work is at present on loan to the Watts Gallery, Compton.

11. Orlando Pursuing the Fata Morgana

Canvas: 65 × 47¼ in, 165 × 120 cm.
Exb.: British Institution, 1848 (95); Arts Council, 1954-5 (76); R.A. Bicentenary (365).
Lit.: M.S.W., I, pp. 64, 234-5, II, pp. 145, 151-2; Chesterton, p. 57; Chapman, repr. Pl. 10; Leicester Catalogue, 1958, pp. 59-60.
Lent by the Leicester Museum and Art Gallery.
Begun at Careggi in 1846, and completed on the artist's return to London; the painting illustrates a passage from Boiardo's *Orlando Inamorato* (Book II, cantos viii-ix). Orlando pursues the fairy, Morgana (who symbolises Fortune or Opportunity) to wrest from her the key to a prison in which she has locked up many other knights. Watts continues the theme, implicit in *Life Illusions* (Tate Gallery) of a man (with chivalric trappings) straining after the alluring form of a naked woman. The painting was presented to the City of Leicester Art Gallery in recognition of the efficiency of the travel agents, Thomas Cook's who organised Watts' visit to Egypt in 1886-7.

12. Found Drowned

Canvas: 57 × 84 in., 145 × 213 cm.
Exb.: Grosvenor Gallery, 1881-2.
Lit.: Barrington, p. 35; M.S.W., I, p. 126; see also Arts Council Catalogue, 1954-5 (28) on the subject.
Lent by the Trustees of the Watts Gallery.
Painted in the Charles Street studio, 1848-50. A suicide lies washed up under the arch of Waterloo Bridge in London. Although close in feeling to Hood's poem *The Bridge of Sighs,* the painting is based on an actual experience, the impact of which was even keener as Watts was living through a period of ill health and mental instability. The work reflects a European preoccupation with Social Realism in the late 1840's e.g. *The Stonebreakers* by Courbet (1849) and *A Scene during the Cholera Epidemic* by J. N. Paton (1849), an artist who exhibited his paintings during this period for the benefit of the unemployed. There is a smaller version of *Found Drowned* in the Walker Art Gallery, Liverpool.

13. Under a Dry Arch

Canvas: 54 × 40 in., 137 × 102 cm.
Exb.: Grosvenor Gallery, 1881-2; Toynbee Hall 1891.
Lit.: Compton Catalogue, I, p. 153; M.S.W., I, p. 126.
Lent by the Trustees of the Watts Gallery.
Painted in 1850 in the Charles Street Studio, and one of the series of paintings that briefly link Watts with the Social Realist Movement in Europe. See also *Found Drowned* (No. 12). The figure of the woman under the arch (later amplified by A. L. Egg in the third canvas of his *Past and Present* series, 1858, Tate Gallery), has the dramatic intensity in pose and expression of the Resurrected Dead in Michelangelo's *Last Judgement* fresco which he first saw in 1845. The subject may be in modern dress, but it also reflects Watts' preoccupation with the eternal sufferings of woman, e.g. *A Scene from Boccaccio* (No. 7).

14. Study for 'Chaos'

Fresco: 40½ × 24 in., 103 × 61 cm.
Coll.: Mrs. R. Barrington.
Exb.: Arts Council, 1954-5 (15).
Lit.: Barrington, pp. 99-102, repr. oppos. p. 68; M.S.W., I, pp. 136, 290-3.
Lent by The Royal Borough of Kensington and Chelsea.
A rare surviving example of Watts' work in true fresco (see also Nos. 8 and 9). This originally formed part of the murals Watts painted for the Prinsep family at Little Holland House, between 1855 and 1860. Although the other decorations were often called 'frescoes', they were in fact largely painted in oils on the dry and unprepared wall's surface. See also *Chaos* (No. 35).

15. Asia Minor

Canvas: 12 × 24 in., 30 × 61 cm.
Lit.: Compton Catalogue, I, p. 10.
Lent by the Trustees of the Watts Gallery.
In October 1856 Watts sailed with Sir Charles Newton's expedition to recover the Mausoleum of Halicarnassus at Budrum. This painting shows the view from the site. Apart from the scenery, Watts was also moved by the colours revealed by excavation that faded almost immediately on contact with the air. Watts returned to England in June 1857.

16. Aileen Spring Rice

Canvas: 16 × 13 in., 41 × 33 cm.
Lit.: Compton Catalogue, II, p. 133.
Lent by the Trustees of the Watts Gallery.
Painted in 1859. The sitter, aged 22, was a sister of the second Lord Monteagle. She married the Hon. J. R. Arthur. Her sister Alice, who was to marry Sir Henry Taylor (No. 20), had been painted by Watts as early as 1839. For much of his career Watts was known chiefly as a portrait painter. He painted friends and celebrities with good grace and great skill. However, he often committed himself to a period of painting commissioned portraits to cover the cost of medical treatment or alterations to his houses.

17. Sir Galahad

Canvas: 21 × 10¼ in., 53 × 26 cm.
Coll.: Louis Huth; C. Handley-Read.
Exh.: Grosvenor Gallery, 1881-2, Maas Gallery, 1963, *English Romantic Paintings* (31).
Lit.: D. Loshak, *Burlington,* 1963, p. 484; J. Maas, *Victorian Painters,* 1969, p. 29.
Lent by Thomas Stainton, Esq.
In this painting, Watts tried to communicate 'the dignity and beauty of purity and chilvalry which things should be the characteristics of the gentleman. . . .' It forms a link between two traditions – the studies of men in armour by painters of an earlier generation such as William Etty and Francis Grant (Watts painted himself in a suit of armour in 1845), and the Arthurian tastes of the Rossetti circle (compare with Rossetti's design for *Sir Galahad at the ruined Chapel* for the Moxon *Tennyson* of 1857 and Burne-Jones' *The Merciful Knight* of 1863). Significantly, one version of *Sir Galahad* was presented to Eton College Chapel. Another is in the Yale collection (78 × 15 in.).

18. Choosing

Panel: 18½ × 14 in., 47 × 35.5 cm.
Coll.: Eustace Smith; Lord Faringdon.
Exh.: R.A., 1864 (395); Arts Council, 1954-5 (37).
Lit.: Barrington, pp. 3, 31; Ellen Terry, *The Story of My Life,* 1908 (large paper edition), repr. p. 150; W. Graham Robertson, 'A Note on Watts' Picture "Choosing" ', *Apollo,* December, 1938, repr. in colour; D. Loshak, *Burlington,* 1963, p. 483, fig. 12.
Lent by Kerrison Preston, Esq.

Watts met the young actress Ellen Terry, then aged 15, in the spring of 1862. He immediately sought to remove her from 'the temptations and abominations of the stage, give her an education and if she continues to have the affection she now feels for me, marry her.' They were married in February, 1864, and within a year, had separated, both parties realising their mutual incompatability. Watts painted her in several guises, e.g. *Watchman, What of the Night* and *Ophelia,* but here he paints her in a far more luxurious context. The plant that she strains to smell is however a camelia, a flower without scent, perhaps sybmolising the empty vanity of the actresses' profession. As a study of a beautiful woman with flowers, this work can be compared with paintings by Rossetti, Burne-Jones and Courbet in the 1860's.

19. Self-Portrait

Canvas: 26 × 21 in., 66 × 53 cm. Signed and dated: *G. F. Watts 1867.*
Coll.: C. H. Rickards; Joseph Rushton; T. H. Ismay; Lord Poltimore.
Exb.: Arts Council, 1954-5 (44).
Lit.: Chapman, repr. Pl. 18.
Lent by Kerrison Preston, Esq.

A portrait that stands between the Compton self-portrait (No 1) and the Uffizi self-portrait as Titian (1879, not in exhibition). He wears a dark velvet coat and a black slouch hat. In his attitude, he preserves that pose of the contemplative pilgrim which is shown in an extraordinary studio photograph of 1854 (Barrington, repro. oppos. p. 32). This shows the artist, gaunt and angular, barefooted and dressed in the full-length robes of the monk. He wears the same slouch hat and clutches a book to his side.

20. Sir Henry Taylor

Canvas: 26½ × 20¾ in., 67 × 53 cm.
Lit.: Compton Catalogue, II, p. 155.
Lent by the Trustees of the Watts Gallery.

A study on a yellow ground, c. 1867, for the portrait in the National Portrait Gallery, of Sir Henry Taylor (1800-1886), the distinguished author, and a constant visitor to Little Holland House in the 1860's, where Watts was a guest of the Prinsep family. Although Watts felt his art compromised by the demands of portraiture, the physiognomy of an intimate or an admired celebrity could provoke real psychological insight. While painting the portrait of W. E. H. Lecky in 1877, Watts maintained that Elizabethan faces had been 'eminently structural, with prominent bone ridges, while from the Restoration to the end of the eighteenth century the bones in faces are almost invisible . . . . Watts found that in the present generation the faces of remarkable men had in a great degree returned to the Elizabethan type'.

21. Evening

Panel: 13 × 14½in., 33 × 37 cm.
Coll.: Mrs. M. Chapman; A. G. B. Russell.
Exb.: Arts Council, 1954–5 (35); Toronto, *The Sacred and Profane in Symbolist Art,* 1969 (16).
Lit.: M.S.W., I, p. 219; Sketchley, p. 165; Barrington, p. 33; Chapman, p. 157; D. Loshak, *Burlington,* 1963, p. 484.
Lent by the Visitors of the Ashmolean Museum, Oxford.
The painting, 1868, is inspired by the artist's sensations from haystacks and trees as he rode home to Little Holland House. Typically he is present in the painting as a knight on horseback. In another version (untraced) Watts replaces the knight with a young labourer leading two grey horses.

22. Time, Death and Judgement

Cardboard: 11¼ × 8¼in., 28.5 × 21 cm.
Coll.: Mrs. M. Chapman; A. G. B. Russell.
Exb.: Arts Council, 1954–5 (36); Sheffield, *Victorian Paintings,* 1968 (116).
Lit.: On the subject: Spielmann, p. 24, repr. p. 23; M.S.W., I, pp. 228, 307, II, p. 86; Cartwright, p. 99, repr. p. 10; West & Pantini, repr. Pl. 52; Chesterton, p. 30; Mrs. Barnett, p. 545.
Lent by the Visitors of the Ashmolean Museum, Oxford.
A subject which Watts grouped with the later modified *House of Life* series of paintings. This is an early sketch, c. 1868, for the composition known in the versions at St. Paul's Cathedral, the Tate Gallery, and the National Gallery of Canada. Watts wrote of the subject, 'Allegory is much out of favour now and by most people condemned, forgetting that spiritual and even most intellectual ideas can only be expressed by similes, and that words themselves are but symbols. The design *Time and Death* is one of several suggestive compositions that I hope to leave behind me in support of my claim to be considered a real artist, and it is by these I wish to be known'. The figure of Time stands to the left, that of Death to the right. The figure of Judgement has not yet been fitted into the composition. In 1882, Canon Barnett wrote that 'the sight of pictures, helped by those who try to interpret the artist, does touch the memories and awaken the hopes of the people. Never in my intercourse with my neighbours have I been so conscious of their souls' needs as when they hung around me listening to what I had to say of Watts' picture *Time, Death and Judgement*'. Watts presented a mosaic replica of the painting to the Church of St. Jude's, Whitechapel.

23. The Wife of Pygmalion

Canvas: 26¼ × 21 in., 67 × 53 cm.
Coll.: Eustace Smith; Sir Alexander Henderson, Bt. (Lord Faringdon).
Exb.: R.A., 1868 (323); Arts Council, 1954–5 (45).
Lit.: W. M. Rossetti and A. C. Swinburne, *Notes on the R.A. Exhibition* 1868, pp. 11-12, 31-2; M.S.W., I, pp. 236, 237-9; Barrington, p. 170; Sketchley, pp. 146-7, repr.; Macmillan, pp. 138-40; Chapman, p. 82.
Lent by the Faringdon Collection Trust.
Painted 1868. Also called *Galatea* and subtitled *A Translation from the Greek,* because it is based on a Greek bust Watts found in the cellars of the Ashmolean Museum, among the Arundel Marbles. As a bustlength study of a beautiful woman against a background of flowers, it can be seen as a more restrained version of *Choosing* (see No. 18), and can be compared with many similar productions by D. G. Rossetti and his circle. This stylistic link with Rossetti may go some way to account for Swinburne's intense admiration for the work, and for Watts' power of making painting and sculpture 'sister arts indeed, yet without invasion or confusion . . .'

24. Orpheus and Eurydice

Canvas: 27½ × 18 in., 70 × 46 cm.
Coll.: A. Macdonald.
Exb.: Grosvenor Gallery, 1879.
Lit.: Barrington, pp. 126-7; G. Reynolds, *Victorian Painting,* 1966, repr. in colour pl. 91.
Lent by Aberdeen Art Gallery.
Painted 1872. Mrs. Barrington described one version of this painting, 'Orpheus too impatient to wait, turns back . . . to see if Eurydice is following him out of Hades. Eurydice is instantly struck and caught back into the shades of the spirit world. . . . In vain, letting fall his lyre, Orpheus encircles her with an arm'. The Orpheus myth had particular relevance for Watts' generation. Chasseriau treated the subject, as did Frederic Leighton. It took on a new importance in the Symbolist Movement, with versions painted by Puvis de Chavannes, Moreau, Redon and Stuck.

25. Denunciation of Cain

Canvas: 58 × 26 in., 147 × 66 cm.
Exb.: Munich, 1893; R.A., Manchester, 1905.
Lit.: M.S.W., I, pp. 258-9; see Arts Council Catalogue, 1954–5 (57) on the subject.
Lent by the Trustees of the Watts Gallery.
Designed c.1868 and completed 1872, at the same time as another version which Watts presented to the Royal Academy on becoming a Member. With the *Eve* series, this is a part of Watts' illustration of the story of Genesis. It was intended by Watts to be included in the later, modified scheme of *The House of Life.* Watts wrote, 'Cain is in my intent on a symbol of reckless, selfish humanity. . . . The denouncing spirits, as I have painted them, represent the voices of conscience reproaching him with the many sins that culminated in the murder. The brand is set upon him; he is shut out from contact with all creation. . . . The brand forbidding human vengeance ('No man shall slay him') constitutes the most terrible part of his punishment; he is driven out from all contact with created things. . . . For him no bird sings, nor flowers bloom, evil passions haunt and follow him, making discords in his ear'.

26. Paolo and Francesca

Canvas: 60 × 51 in., 152 × 129.5 cm.
Exb.: Arts Council, 1954-5 (59).
Lit.: West & Pantini, repr. Pl. 12; *Grosvenor Gallery Notes,* 1879, p. 28; Alston (33), repr. Pl. xiv; Barrington, pp. 125-6; Chapman, p. 103.
Lent by the Trustees of the Watts Gallery.
This is a variant of the design painted up for exhibition at the British Institution in 1848. For their sin, the lovers whirl through eternity. The composition is strongly influenced by Ary Scheffer's painting of the identical scene, available in many versions, e.g. one in the Wallace Collection, dated 1835. Scheffer was a friend of Lady Duff Gordon. Loshak, Arts Council Catalogue, 1954-5 (59), identifies Francesca as Virginia Pattle, Mrs. Prinsep's sister, with whom Watts was said to have been in love.

27. The Judgement of Paris

Canvas: 31½ × 25¾ in., 80 × 65 cm.
Coll.: Louis Miller; Lord Faringdon; Sotheby's June 13, 1934.
Exb.: Paris, *Exposition Universelle,* 1878 (265); R.A., 1905 (230).
Lit.: M.S.W., II, p. 45; Catalogue of the Faringdon Collection, 1964, p. 17.
Lent by the Faringdon Collection Trust.
This picture, studied from the artist's favourite model 'Long Mary', was nearing completion in 1872, and was completed in 1874. Watts would undoubtedly have known of Etty's version of the subject (1825), and also Flaxman's, plate 27 of the *Iliad* series. But Watts has here chosen to represent the three goddesses who appeared to Paris, without their attributes, concentrating instead on the harmonies of their robes. See also *Olympus on Ida* (No. 38).

28. Love and Death

Canvas: 59½ × 29½ in., 151 × 75 cm. Signed and dated: *G. F. Watts, 1875.*
Coll.: C. T. Galloway; Lord Winterstoke.
Exb.: Manchester, 1874; Arts Council, 1954-5 (60); Brighton, *Death, Heaven and the Victorians* 1970, (37).
Lit.: M.S.W., I, p. 283 and 283m.; C. E. Hallé, *Notes from a painter's life,* 1909, pp. 215-7; J. L. Sweeney (ed) Henry James: *The Painter's Eye,* 1956, p. 142; H. T. Moore (ed) *The Collected Letters of D. H. Lawrence,* 1962, I, p. 47; *Strand Magazine,* July, 1901.
Lent by Bristol City Art Gallery.
The first of eight versions, the initial idea came to Watts in 1862 when he heard of the death of the young Marquis of Lothian. One version was shown at Whitechapel. Canon Barnett wrote of Watts, 'He lent many of his pictures and by his own faith made faith'. When reviewing the work, Henry James described how a 'figure, with its back to the spectator, and with a sinister sweep of garment and gesture, prepares to pass across a threshold where, beside a rosebush that has shed its flowers, a boy figure of love staggers forth, and, with head and body reverted in entreaty, tries in vain to bar its entrance'. D. H. Lawrence admired 'the blurred idea that Death is shrouded, but a dark embracing mother, who slops over us, and frightens us because we are children'. Watts may have known Gustave Moreau's *Young Man and Death,* 1865 Salon, painted in memory of Chasseriau, who died in 1856, aged 37.

29. Ariadne in Naxos

Canvas: 29½ × 37 in., 75 × 94 cm. Signed and dated: *G. F. Watts 1875.*
Coll.: C. H. Rickards; Lord Davey; C. Morland Agnew; M. Samuel.
Exb.: Manchester, 1880; Arts Council, 1954-5 (62); Paris, 1972 (321); Newcastle, *Albert Moore and his Contemporaries,* 1972 (128).
Lit.: M.S.W., I, pp. 236, 283; Macmillan, pp. 133-5; Sketchley, p 143; *Connoisseur,* July 1918, repr. p. 168; J. Maas, *Victorian Painters,* 1969, p. 17, repr. in colour.
Lent by the Guildhall Art Gallery.
Described by Watts as 'the most complete picture I have painted'. Ariadne, the daughter of King Minos of Crete, was abandoned by her lover Theseus on the island of Naxos. The leopards in the right hand corner of Watts' picture, and the gesture of the attendant, indicate the arrival of Dionysius, who was to soothe away her sorrow with drink and fun. The composition is strongly influenced by Titian's *Bacchus and Ariadne* (National Gallery, London); the drapery style reflects the contemporary interest in the sculptural surfaces of the Elgin Marbles. Other versions are in the Walker Art Gallery, Liverpool, and the Fogg Art Museum, Cambridge, Mass. The subject was a particular favourite with British artists. Examples exhibited at the Royal Academy include those by M. A. Shee (1834), A. Geddes (1844), A. Cooper (1848), F. Leighton (1868) and W. B. Richmond (1872).

30. Freshwater

Canvas: 26 × 21 in., 66 × 53 cm.
Exb.: Grosvenor Gallery, 1881-2.
Lit.: Compton Catalogue, I, p. 58; Bayes, pl. XIII.
Lent by the Trustees of the Watts Gallery.
Painted in 1875 from Watts' room in The Briary, the house built for the Prinseps on the Isle of Wight when Thoby Prinsep left Little Holland House. The local community included Alfred Tennyson, Julia Margaret Cameron, the photographer, and Watts' dear friend, Mrs. Nassau Senior. Watts liked the area for its mild climate.

31. The Carrara Mountains

Silk Laid on Canvas: 32 × 45½ in., 81 × 115.5 cm.
Coll.: Lord Davey; J. F. Cheetham; Sir L. Jones.
Exb.: Grosvenor Gallery, 1881 (72); Arts Council, 1954-5 (66).
Lit.: Cartwright, p. 19; Macmillan, pp. 94-6.
Lent by Mrs. Charlotte Frank.
Watts first painted this view of the Carrara Mountains in watercolours, from the Tower of Pisa, in c. 1845-6. From these studies he made two paintings during the period 1875-81. The other is in the collection of the Ashmolean Museum, Oxford. Watts had suddenly and enthusiastically turned to landscape studies in May 1845, after finishing an ambitious fresco in the Hollands' Villa at Careggi.

32. When Poverty Comes in the Door, Love Flies out the Window

Panel: 15 × 19¾ in., 38 × 50 cm.
Coll.: Mrs. M. Chapman.
Exb.: Carlisle, *Victorian Painters,* 1970 (17).
Lit.: Barrington, p. 137.
Lent by Carlisle Art Gallery.

A study, c. 1879, for the larger work (London art market, 1961, not traced). Watts wrote, 'You will see that carelessness and indifference to domestic duties, shown by general disorder, doors of cupboards hanging by broken hinges, etc. – have in reality left the door open to the intruder . . .' a symbolic programme unusually explicit in Watts' *oeuvre.* The composition is one usually associated with the eighteenth century erotic print, e.g. Le Barbier's *La Prudence en Defaut,* or Hogarth's *The Death of the Earl* from the *Marriage a la Mode* series, which show the lovers surprised by the husband.

33. The Titans

Canvas: 15¾ × 24 in., 40 × 61 cm.
Coll.: A. Fisher; C. Handley-Read.
Exb.: R.A., *The Handley-Read Collection,* 1972, (C.72).
Lit.: See 1972 R.A. Catalogue.
Lent by Thomas Stainton, Esq.

A study for two of the 'gigantic figures stretched out at full length' in *Chaos* (see No. 35). Both works show how Watts continued to explore the formal possibilities of the early *House of Life* designs. The description in the introduction for this project is a version which Mrs. Watts wrote from rough notes Watts had written.

34. The Court of Death

Canvas: 25¾ × 17¾ in., 65 × 45 cm.
Coll.: Presented by Mrs. Watts to the Castle Museum, Norwich, 1907.
Exb.: R.A., 1905 (150); Dublin and Manchester, *W. B. Yeats Exhibition,* 1961 (122).
Lit.: See M.S.W., index.
Lent by the City of Norwich Museums.

The subject was originally conceived as a decoration for a proposed mortuary chapel for London paupers, and was grouped by Watts with others in *The House of Life* series. The first completed design (1868-81) is at the Walker Art Gallery, Liverpool. The large version (167 × 108 in., Tate Gallery) was begun in the 1870's but never completed. Watts described the work, 'Death the sovereign power, holding in her lap an infant form that has been claimed before its life had well begun, a symbol that the beginning and end of life lies in the lap of Death, is seated enthroned upon the ruins of the world. On either side stand the two angel figures, guarding the portals of the Unknown beyond the Grave, and at her feet are gathered all sorts and conditions of men, who have come to render their last homage to the Universal Queen' e.g. the warrior, the nobleman, the cripple. The winding sheet is embraced by a young girl and played with by an unsuspecting babe.

35. Chaos

Canvas: 7⅞ × 29¼ in., 19 × 74 cm.
Coll.: Watts Collection, Compton; by deed of exchange to Fitzwilliam Museum, Cambridge.
Lit.: M.S.W., I, pp. 102-3.
Lent by Fitzwilliam Musuem, Cambridge.

Part of the original *House of Life* project (see catalogue introduction), a great hall to be painted in fresco with a programme of Watts' own devising. It shows something of the original idea for 'a number of gigantic figures stretched out at full length' that were to represent a range of mountains, but was painted much later in c.1882. Watts came to regret the title, preferring *Cosmos* or *Chaos passing into Cosmos*. The composition was suggested by cracks and stains on the dirty plaster of a wall. In the same way *The Sower of the Systems* grew in his mind from patterns of light on the ceiling.

36. Tasting the First Oyster or B.C.

Canvas: 41 × 65 in., 104 × 165 cm.
Exb.: Liverpool, 1884; Whitechapel, 1895.
Lit.: Compton Catalogue, I. p. 14.
Lent by The Trustees of the Watts Gallery.

Other British artists found some relief from the earnestness of purpose expected of them in boisterousness outside the studio. Incapable of this, Watts produced a series of paintings 'purposely intended to raise a smile', such as *The Cowl maketh not the Monk* (No. 44). The bovine grotesqueness of the scene can be compared with contemporary pictorial jokes such as H. S. Marks' *A Medieval Toothache,* and mythological scenes by Böcklin and Stuck. It is particularly close in feeling to evocations of prehistoric life by Felix Cormon, e.g. *The Flight of Cain* (1880) and *Return from the Hunt* (1884). Watts later came to regret painting a joke on such a large scale. The work was painted in 1885 and shown at Whitechapel in 1895, where Canon Barnett's exhibitions at the old school-house were very popular, 'crowds flooded in, and anxiety was often felt to prevent crushing and damage . . .'. From 1901, exhibitions were held in the new Art Gallery.

37. Mammon

Canvas: 21 × 12½ in., 53 × 32 cm. Signed: *G. F. Watts.*
Exb.: Arts Council, 1954-5 (69).
Lit.: M.S.W., II, p. 149; Chesterton, 108-13, 115 (Tate version repr.); Shrewsbury, 113-18 (Tate version repr.).
Lent by the Trustees of the Watts Gallery.

An oil study, 1882-3, for the large painting in the Tate Gallery (71½ × 41½ in., 1884-5). Watts constantly inveighed against what he called 'Mammon-worship' – the desire to 'get on', – 'characteristics of the age I cannot but deplore'. At one stage, Watts half-seriously suggested setting up a statue of Mammon in Hyde Park where worshippers of 'Holy Mammon – Divine Respectability – Sacred Dividend' could kneel. In 1897, Canon Barnett wrote after walking through London, 'What is possible when houses are so close, the air so thick, and when people love to have it so! It seemed as if Watts were right and Mammon were God'.

38. Olympus on Ida

Canvas: 25½ × 21 in., 65 × 53 cm.
Exh.: R.A., 1905; Arts Council, 1954-5 (71).
Lit.: M.S.W., II, pp. 45, 57, repr., III, oppos. p. 234 repro.; K. Preston, 'A Note on Watts' Picture "Olympus on Ida"', *Apollo,* February, 1947 (Preston version repr.).
Lent by the Trustees of the Watts Gallery.
See Note for *The Judgement of Paris* (No. 27). Watts particularly admired this canvas for its 'opalesque' quality which, with further work, might have been lost. This painting (1885) can be compared with other groupings of female figures in classical robes, e.g. Frederic Leighton's *Greek Girls picking up Pebbles* (1871) and Albert Moore's *Waiting to Cross* (1888). There is another version in the Kerrison Preston collection. In 1890, Watts wrote, 'I have tried to express without attributes the different characteristics . . . to suggest a certain sense of the celestial perfume accompanying them'.

39. Ararat

Canvas: 34¾ × 15¾ in., 88 × 40 cm.
Coll.: The Misses Colman.
Exh.: Melbourne, 1889; Southwark, 1895.
Lit.: Bayes, pl. 4; Muther III, p. 635.
Lent by York City Art Gallery.
Watts painted many subjects to do with the Deluge, such as *Building the Ark* of 1862-3, and *The Dove that returned* of 1868-9. In this painting Watts sought to convey something of the loneliness and austerity of the place where the ark came to rest, with the simplest possible means. There is another version (46 × 27 in.) once in the collection of W. Carver, present whereabouts unknown.

40. Dweller in the Innermost

Canvas: 41¾ × 27½ in., 106 × 70 cm.
Exh.: Grosvenor Gallery, 1886.
Lit.: Tate Gallery Catalogue, 1929, p. 409; W. Crane, *An Artist's Reminiscences,* 1907, p. 252.
Lent by the Trustees of the Tate Gallery.
The figure, holding the silver trumpet of Truth, and with winged arrows in her lap, symbolises the concept of Conscience. A bright star shines from her head, and her body describes the triangle of the Trinity in a mandorla of light. The artist himself did not encourage a literal interpretation, 'I myself can hardly give a mental form to the confused ideas which it endeavours in some slight way to focus, vague murmurings rather than fancies which constantly beat me and prevent any kind of work. . . .'

41. The Sphinx

Canvas: 15½ × 20 in., 39 × 51 cm.
Lit.: Compton Catalogue, I, p. 135.
Lent by the Trustees of the Watts Gallery.
Painted from many studies in watercolour and oil made on the spot during his visit to Egypt in 1886-7 (see Nos. 69 and 70). At the time, Watts wrote of the Sphinx, 'An epitome of all Egyptian art, its solemnity – mystery – infinity.' The work reflects more the Symbolist fascination with the Sphinx as ineffable mystery, than a purely topographical interest, e.g. Holman Hunt's *The Sphinx* (1854, Harris Museum, Preston).

42. Samuel Augustus Barnett

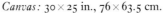

Canvas: 30 × 25 in., 76 × 63.5 cm.
Coll.: Mrs. Barnett.
Exb.: Whitechapel, 1901; Hampstead (date unknown).
Lit.: Compton Catalogue, II, p. 9; Mrs. Barnett, p. 378.
Lent by the Trustees of the National Portrait Gallery.
The sitter was Canon Samuel Barnett (1844-1913), the founder and Warden of Toynbee Hall, the Vicar of St. Jude's Church, Whitechapel, and later Canon of Westminster. The portrait was painted in 1887 as a tribute to the Canon's work among the poor in Whitechapel. In a letter to a friend, Canon Barnett wrote, 'On Monday we went to Watts; he finished my portrait and gave it to my wife. She is very pleased and the face is certainly like something in me. He was very happy in her pleasure, and she was very happy in her possession'. The painter William Rothenstein remembers the Barnetts in the 1880's, 'beginning to organise exhibitions of paintings with the warm support of Watts, Burne-Jones and Holman Hunt who freely lent their pictures. The Barnetts had, I fancy, but slender funds at their disposal, on which account we acted by turns as warders while the exhibitions were on'.

43. Progress

Canvas: 42 × 22 in., 107 × 56 cm.
Coll.: The Misses Colman.
Exb.: R.S.B.A., 1890; New Gallery, 1904; Manchester, Newcastle, Edinburgh, 1905.
Lit.: M.S.W., II, pp. 303, 313; Shrewsbury, p. 79 and repr. oppos.
Lent by York City Art Gallery.
Having just begun the painting in 1888, Watts wrote, 'The rider on the white horse must represent the progress of spiritual and intellectual ideals'. On the ground are four figures – the old philosopher so buried in his book as to be unaware of the blazing light, the money-grubber, the sluggard, and one young man who is aware of the challenge of the vision. There is a larger version, begun 1902, and measuring 111 × 56½ in. at Compton.

44. The Cowl Maketh not the Monk

Canvas: 44½ × 24½ in., 113 × 62 cm.
Coll.: Lady Rothschild.
Exb.: R.A., 1889; New Gallery, 1896.
Lit.: M.S.W., II, p. 141; Chesterton, repr. frontispiece.
Lent by the County Borough of Bournemouth Art Gallery and Museums.
Painted in 1889, also known as *The Habit does not make the Monk.* This is
Watts' response to the criticism that he had no sense of humour. The
composition appears to be based on Anna Lea Merrit's *Love Locked Out*
(1884, Tate Gallery) and, more distantly Holman Hunt's *The Light of the
World.* This has been refurbished with the heavy humour of German
painters of whimsy such as Schwind and Richter. Watts was very fond of
this type of simpering *amorino*, e.g. *Good Luck to your Fishing* (1889) and
Trifles light as Air (1901) (neither in exhibition).

45. Sic Transit

Canvas: 40½ × 80½ in., 103 × 204 cm.
Exb.: New Gallery, 1892; Munich, 1893; Edinburgh, 1896.
Lit.: M.S.W., II, pp. 197, 199; Barrington, p. 38; Tate Catalogue, 1929,
p. 410.
Lent by the Trustees of the Tate Gallery.
Begun in 1891, and completed the next year. Watts wrote, 'The shrouded
figure is the symbol of human life ended, with all its possibilities laid
away'. At the foot of the bier are emblems of human life at its noblest, the
peacock plumed casque of the warrior, the scallop shell of the wanderer,
the lute of the musician, the book of the scholar, the roses of love, etc.
This was one of 22 works by Watts exhibited with the Society of Artists
in Munich in 1893. Those, who were more familiar with the sensuousness
of Rossetti's art, were disappointed with the 'sobriety of his colour, his
preference for subdued tones, his distaste for all "dexterity" and freedom
from all calculated refinement. . . .' (Muther III p. 642).

46. Creation of Eve

Canvas: 31 × 12½ in., 79 × 32 cm.
Coll.: Sir George Drummond.
Lit.: M.S.W., I, p. 262, II, pp. 45, 138-141, 183; Barrington, pp. 136-7.
Lent by the Trustees of the Lady Lever Art Gallery.
Painted c. 1892. *Creation of Eve, Eve Tempted* and *Eve Penitent* were
intended by the artist to be included in *The House of Life* as it became in
the 1870's, a series of easel paintings hanging together without the
iconographic programme of 1848. Watts wrote of the *Eve* trilogy as an
attempt to show 'the three stages through which human life has to pass.
In the first, the newly created soul is more conscious of heaven than of
earth, the hands are spread out, they grasp nothing of earth's treasures;
the fact alone is firmly planted. In the second stage the sway of the senses
has descended upon the soul. . . . In the third – Eve Repentant – all is
changed, the earthly paradise is wrecked'.

47. Love and Life

Canvas: 86¼ × 47¾ in., 219 × 121 cm. Signed and dated: *G. F. Watts 1893.*
Exb.: Melbourne, 1888.
Lit.: M.S.W., II, pp. 234-5 and index; Barrington, pp. 129-30.
Lent by Musee du Louvre, Paris.
'I would suggest frail and feeble human existence aided to ascend from the lower to the higher plane by Love with his wide wings of sympathy, charity, tenderness, and human affection. Love is not intended to be either personal or carnal' (Watts, MS note, Compton catalogue). This version was chosen by Leon Bénédite to be purchased by the French nation for the Luxembourg Museum. The painting was eventually presented by Watts to the museum. Another version, when on loan to the South Kensington Museum, was powerful enough to convert the French critic Robert de la Sizeranne to the validity of allegory and myth (*Revue de Deux Mondes,* quoted Compton Catalogue).

48. The Sower of the Systems

Canvas: 26 × 21 in., 66 × 53 cm.
Exb.: Arts Council, 1954-5 (84); Paris, 1972 (323).
Lit.: Compton Catalogue, I, p. 134; M.S.W., II, pp. 105, 302; Macmillan, p. 288; Alston (111).
Lent by the Trustees of the Watts Gallery.
The inspiration for this painting of unknown cosmic energy and creation was the patterns made by a night light on the ceiling above. Watts likened this attempt at painting the unpaintable to a child's attempt to draw God. The child drew 'a great number of circular scribbles, and putting his paper on a soft surface, struck his pencil through the centre, making a great void. This was utterly absurd as a picture, but there was a greater idea in it than in Michelangelo's old man with a beard'.

49. Endymion

Canvas: 41 × 48 in., 104 × 122 cm.
Exb.: R.A., 1904; R.A., Manchester, and Newcastle, 1905.
Lit.: See Arts Council catalogue, 1954-5 (58) on the subject; J. Golding, *Duchamp: The Bride stripped Bare,* 1973, p. 91; this version, M.S.W., II, p. 313.
Lent by the Trustees of the Watts Gallery.
'Endymion loved the moon, who is here represented under the form of Diana, in pale blue robes, descending from heaven, and embracing him as he sleeps on the ground' (Watts' description, printed in the 1905 Catalogue). Watts was working on this version in 1869. He took it up again in 1903 to make it more visionary and mystic than the earlier version of 1873 (Lord Glenconner coll.). The composition may have been drawn from one of William Blake's illustrations to Blair's *The Grave* (1808) entitled *The Soul hovering over the Body.* The figure of Diana closely resembles Auguste Preault's *Ophelia* (1843, exhibited 1850 Salon). In the pose of Endymion, Watts preserves something of the Theseus figure in the Elgin Marbles.

50. Evening Landscape

Canvas: 16 × 12 in., 41 × 30 cm.
Coll.: Bequeathed by Cecil French to the Watts Gallery.
Lent by the Trustees of the Watts Gallery.
One of the fresh and evocative landscape studies Watts made of the Surrey Countryside. It was painted in 1903.

51. Green Summer

Canvas: 66 × 35½ in., 168 × 90 cm.
Exb.: New Gallery, and Liverpool, 1903; Manchester, Newcastle, Edinburgh, 1905; Dublin, 1906.
Lit.: W. Bayes, Pl. XI repr.; M.S.W., II, pp. 312-3.
Lent by the Trustees of the Watts Gallery.
Watts intended to study 'the variety to be found in the full green of summer'. It shows the view from the studio at Limnerslease, the house he had built in Compton, near Guildford. Around the time this was painted, Watts said, 'The desire in me to paint landscape grows, I want to paint landscapes more and more'. Completed in 1903, he had worked on it for 5 or 6 years. Canon Barnett and his wife visited Limnerslease in March, 1896. 'We found them established on a hillside amid the fir trees with peeps towards Hindhead. Their house just teems with art and ideas. . . . He and she were, as ever, humble, inspired, and devoted.'

52. Surrey Woodland, End of the Day

Canvas: 30 × 25 in., 76 × 63.5 cm.
Lent by the Trustees of the Watts Gallery.
One of the group of landscape studies Watts made of the countryside around him at Limnerslease. See also *Green Summer* (No. 51).

DRAWINGS AND OIL SKETCHES

53. Studies for Cricketing Lithographs

Pencil heightened with chalk: each 11 × 9 in., 28 × 23 cm.
Coll.: Given by Watts to the M.C.C. in 1895.
Lit.: M.S.W., I, pp. 28–30, on the subject.
Lent by the Cricket Memorial Gallery, Marylebone Cricket Club.
Drawn c.1837–8, as illustrations to *Felix on the Bat*, a book on cricket by
Nicholas Wanostrocht ('Nicholas Felix'). Watts shows 'Felix' himself,
Fuller Pilch, and Alfred Mynn, in the various positions of the cricketer,
The Cut, Leg ½ Volley, Forward, The Draw, and *Play.* There were
originally 7 plates in the series. Wanostrocht was also famous for the
machine he invented to replace the bowler at net practice. Watts was much
in his company at this time. Wanostrocht ran a progressive school at
Blackheath where Watts often visited him. Watts' drawings of cricketers
were far from being regarded as ephemera. Years later a friend stopped
in front of one of the original drawings which he saw by candlelight on a
darkened staircase. 'Only Watts could have drawn that leg!' he exclaimed.

54, 55. Studies of a Couple Embracing on a Parapet

Pen and ink:
each 6½ × 8⅛ *in.,*
16 × 20.5 cm.
Lent by
Brinsley Ford, Esq.
Perhaps studies for
a *Romeo and Juliet*
composition, which
was never carried
out.

56. Julia Margaret Cameron

Pencil: 7 × 4½ in., 18 × 11 cm.
Coll.: Mrs. M. Chapman.
Exb.: Arts Council, 1954-5 (117).
Lent by Brinsley Ford, Esq.
Watts painted Mrs. Cameron's portrait in 1852. This sketch relates to it.
The sitter was a sister of Watts' friend Mrs. Prinsep. She was celebrated
as a photographer. Watts greatly admired her work.

57. Sketches for a Composition

Red chalk: 7⅛ × 5¼ in., 18 × 13 cm.
Coll.: Mrs. M. Chapman.
Exb.: Arts Council, 1954-5 (124).
Lent by Brinsley Ford, Esq.
Perhaps a study for a mural Watts painted at 7, Carlton House Terrace
for the Lord Somers, and called *Battle of Gods and Giants* (1856).

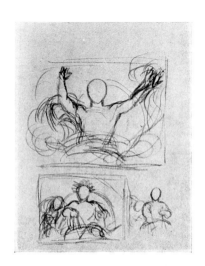

58. Seated Woman Reading a Newspaper

Pencil: 7¼ × 4½ in., 18 × 11 cm.
Coll.: Mrs. M. Chapman.
Exb.: Arts Council, 1954-5 (117).
Lent by Brinsley Ford, Esq.
Perhaps a study of one of the Pattle sisters (Mrs. Jackson, Mrs. Prinsep, Mrs. Cameron, Mrs. Dalrymple, Countess Somers). Beneath is a drapery study. Drawn on India Office paper given him by Thoby Prinsep who worked there.

59. Standing Woman with Right Hand on Chair, with Study of Left Hand

Black chalk on brown paper: 18 × 12⅝ in., 45.5 × 32 cm.
Coll.: Mrs. Watts; T. Lowinsky.
Lent by Brinsley Ford, Esq.

60. Two Figure Studies in Classical Dress

Black chalk heightened with white on brown paper: 10 × 9¼ in., 25.5 × 23.5 cm.
Lent by Brinsley Ford, Esq.

61. Studies for 'The Sacrifice of Noah'

Pencil: 8¼ × 10½ in., 21 × 27 cm.
Coll.: Mrs. M. Chapman.
Exb.: Arts Council, 1954-5 (132).
Lent by Brinsley Ford, Esq.
During the early 1860's many British artists were commissioned to produce drawings to be engraved on wood by the Dalziel Brothers, and produced as an Illustrated Bible. As well as this subject Watts also prepared *Noah building the Ark* and *Esau meeting Jacob.* The Illustrated Bible project failed but the plates alone were published in 1880.

62. Two Studies of Horse's Head

Red chalk: 9⅞ × 7⅛ in., 25 × 18 cm.
Lent by Brinsley Ford, Esq.

63. Studies of a Dog

Pencil: 8 × 9 in., 20 × 23 cm.
Coll.: Mrs. M. Chapman.
Exb.: Arts Council, 1954-5 (138).
Lent by Brinsley Ford, Esq.

64. Suggestion of the Bed Curtain

Ink wash: 6⅛ × 4 in., 15.5 × 10 cm. Iscr: *Suggest by Bed curtain when staying with Dr. Cheyne at Brighton* (in Watts' hand).
Coll.: Mrs. M. Chapman.
Exb.: Arts Council, 1954-5 (145).
Lent by Brinsley Ford, Esq.
While recuperating in Brighton from the effects of over-work Watts was kicked in the shins by a horse. This study may have been done while he was laid up in bed.

65. Study of a Female Nude

Black chalk heightened with white on brown paper: 16¼ × 5¾ in., 41 × 14.5 cm.
Lent by Brinsley Ford, Esq.

66. Hope

Sanguine: 53½ × 42 in., 136 × 107 cm.
Lit.: See Arts Council catalogue, 1954-5 (65) on the subject.
Lent by the Trustees of the Watts Gallery.
In 1885, Watts wrote, 'I am painting a picture of Hope sitting on a globe with bandaged eyes, playing on a lyre which has all the strings broken but one . . . listening with all her might to the little sound'. Watts' image of *Hope* – it was widely reproduced – has always had peculiar relevance. Mrs. Watts tells the story of a man whose life was given new purpose by contemplating it; in 1889, during the great dock strike, John Burns, one of the dockers' leaders, asked Canon Barnett to explain its symbolism to him: reproductions of the paintings were given to Egyptian troops after their defeat in the 1967 War. The version here exhibited is uncharacteristically Rossettian in flavour, and may have been worked upon by Cecil Schott. Watts' first design dates from 1865-70. The most famous version, in the Tate Gallery, was completed in 1886. The single figure of a naked woman symbolic of Hope was also used by Puvis de Chavannes (c.1871) and G. Klimt (1903).

67. The Bay of Salamis

Oil sketch on paper: 6 × 13½ in., 15 × 34 cm. Inscr. on reverse: *Bay of Salamis, 1887* (in Watts' hand).
Coll.: Mrs. M. Chapman.
Exb.: Arts Council, 1954-5 (150).
Lit.: M.S.W., II, p. 74.
Lent by Brinsley Ford, Esq.
In 1886, Watts married his second wife, Mary Fraser-Tytler. They went on a honeymoon cruise to Malta, Egypt, Athens and Constantinople. This work was painted on the way from Alexandria to Athens in the early spring of 1887. Mrs. Watts wrote, 'The bay of Salamis was blue to its depths, blue poured into a cup of gold; the sky was blue, not that of a dye nor a paint, but as if fold over fold of some ethereal web was laid over and over again to infinity'. Watts said that 'if I could paint that, I feel it would be worth a lifetime, a lifetime of work. . . .' See also *Salamis* (No. 68).

68. Salamis

Canvas: 6 × 13½ in., 15 × 34 cm.
Lent by the Trustees of the Watts Gallery.
See note to *The Bay of Salamis* (No. 67).

69. Egypt

Oil Sketch on paper: 6¾ × 13¾ in., 17 × 35 cm. Inscr. on reverse: *Egypt* (in Watts' hand).
Coll.: Mrs. M. Chapman.
Exb.: Arts Council, 1954-5 (149).
Lent by Brinsley Ford, Esq.
Painted on the artist's visit to Egypt with his new bride, 1886-7. This is a study of the sandstone cliffs seen from the boat. Mrs. Watts recorded that her husband noticed how in their structural formation they 'had suggested to the early builder the form of the pylon and the pyramid'.

70. Egypt

Canvas: 6½ × 13½ in., 16.5 × 34 cm.
Lent by the Trustees of the Watts Gallery.
The Middle East held particular fascination for the British artist, e.g. David Roberts, J. F. Lewis, F. Goodall and Holman Hunt. The journey up the Nile was a favourite occupation. Thomas Seddon and Edward Lear sailed in 1853, Frederic Leighton sailed as far as Phylae in 1867. Watts could only venture as far as Assouan because of political turmoil in the area. See note to *Egypt* (No. 69).

71. Clouds over the Alps

Water-colour and gouache: 6⅞ × 7⅞ in., 17 × 20 cm.
Coll.: Mrs. M. Chapman.
Exb.: Arts Council, 1954-5 (152).
Lit.: M.S.W., II, p. 126.
Lent by Brinsley Ford, Esq.
Watts and his wife spent the winter and spring of 1887-8 abroad to escape the English fogs. This study probably records a view seen on the journey from Aix-les-Bains to Monnetier. Mrs. Watts writes of the scene, 'as the train drew up at a little station called La Roche-sur-Foron, steeped in the crimson of the setting sun, suddenly a line of snowy peaks blazed out upon a background of giant cumulus clouds. Before there was time for the least change to dim these glories, we were whirled away, still speechless with astonishment. . . .'

SCULPTURE

72. Physical Energy

Bronze: 22 (high) including plinth × 19¾ × 9¼ in., 56 × 50 × 23 cm.
Exb.: Arts Council, 1954-5 (158).
Lit.: M.S.W., III, p. 270 and repr. oppos.; R. Gutch, *G. F. Watts' Sculpture, Burlington Magazine,* 1968, December, pp. 693-9. For the small model see M.S.W., I, pp. 256-7; Barrington, p. 49.
Lent by Kerrison Preston, Esq.
A small model executed about 1870, and later worked up into a large version which remained unfinished at the artist's death. Casts of the full-scale work can be seen in Kensington Gardens, London, and as part of the Cecil Rhodes Memorial near Cape Town. there is a third cast in Salisbury, Rhodesia. Later in his life, Watts described, the concept in terms that link it with *The House of Life* project. This was Man as he ought to be, 'a part of creation, of cosmos in fact, his great limbs to be akin to the rocks and to the roots, and his head to be as the sun'. Specifically, Watts tried to symbolise that activity which 'is impelling man to undertake a new enterprise. The horse restrained by the hand, which as if on the tiller of a rudder, is not reining it back. This is a symbol of something done for the time, while the rider looks out for the next thing to do. The incline of the plinth is slightly symbolic of a rising wave'. The bronze version exhibited here was made by T. H. Wren after Watts' death.

NOTES BY CHRIS MULLEN

APPENDIX I
Selected Reading List on G. F. Watts

PRIMARY SOURCES

R. Alston, *The Mind and Works of G. F. Watts, O.M., R.A.*, 1929 (Alston).
Anon, *The Masterpieces of G. F. Watts*, 1918.
Anon, *The New Associates of the Royal Academy, Illustrated London News*, March 9, 1867, p.239. (I.L.N.).
Anon, *G. F. Watts, Magazine of Art*, Vol. 1, 1878, p.241.
Anon, *Physical Energy, Cape Town, Illustrated London News*, November 21, 1906, p.723.
Arts Council exhibition catalogue, *G. F. Watts*, 1954-5.
Mrs R. Barrington, *G. F. Watts, Reminiscences*, 1905 (Barrington).
W. Bayes, *The Landscapes of G. F. Watts*, undated (W. Bayes).
W. Blunt, *G. F. Watts*, The Master Series, No. 37.
J. Cartwright, *G. F. Watts R.A., Art Journal Easter Annual*, 1896.
R. Chapman, *The Laurel and the Thorn*, 1945 (Chapman).
G. K. Chesterton, *G. F. Watts*, 1904. (Chesterton).
H. Corkran, *Note on G. F. Watts, Portfolio*, 1878, p.129.
S. Erskine, *The Memorial Gallery at Limnerslease, Studio*, Vol. 38, 1906, p.189.
R. Fry, *G. F. Watts, Burlington*, Vol. 5, 1904, p.452.
R. E. Gutch, *G. F. Watts' Sculpture, Burlington*, December, 1968, p.693.
The Earl of Ilchester, *Chronicles of Holland House*, 1937.
D. Loshak, *G. F. Watts and Ellen Terry, Burlington*, November, 1963, p.476.
H. Macmillan, *The Life-work of George Frederick Watts, R.A.*, 1903 (Macmillan).
W. B. Richmond, *G. F. Watts, Nineteenth Century and After*, Vol. 157, 1905, p.427.
C. Ricketts, *Watts at Burlington House, Burlington*, Vol. 6, 1905, p.346.
O. von Schleinitz, *George Frederick Watts*, Velhagen & Klasing, 1904.
H. W. Shrewsbury, *The Visions of an Artist*, 1918 (Shrewsbury).
R. Sketchley, *Watts*, 1905 (Sketchley).
M. H. Spielmann, *The Work of G. F. Watts, Pall Mall Gazette Extra*, 1886.
M. S. Watts, *George Frederick Watts*, 3 Vols., 1912 (M.S.W.).
W. K. West and R. Pantini, *G. F. Watts*, 1904.

In preparation: a new biography by Wilfrid Blunt.

SECONDARY SOURCES

O. R. Agresti, *Giovanni Costa*, 1907.
T. J. Clark, *The Absolute Bourgeois: Artists and Politics in France, 1848-51*, 1973.
S. C. Colvin, *Memories and Notes*, 1921.
C. W. Cope, *Reminiscences*, 1891.
Exhibition catalogue, *La peintre romantique anglaise et les pre-raphealites*, Paris, Petit Palais, 1972 (Paris).
W. Gaunt, *Victorian Olympus*, 1952.
G. D. Leslie, *The Inner Life of the Royal Academy*, 1914.
R. Muther, *The History of Modern Painting*, 3 vols, 1896 (Muther).
W. M. Rossetti, *Fine Art Chiefly Contemporary*, 1867.
W. M. Rossetti, *Some Reminiscences*, 1906.
W. Rothenstein, *Men and Memories*, I, 1931.
L. Troubridge, *Memories and Reflections*, 1925.

WATTS AND MURAL PAINTING

Art Journal, September 1, 1861, p.286, *St. James the Less, Westminster*, see also *Illustrated London News*, February 1, 1862, p.122.
Art Journal, January 1, 1866, p.10, the South Kensington lunette.
A. H. Church, *Cleaning a Fresco, Portfolio*, 1891, p.48.
Illustrated London News, July 17, 1847, p.40, *Alfred Inciting the Saxons*.
A. L. Baldry, *Modern Mural Decoration* 1902.
T. S. R. Boase *The decoration of the New Palace of Westminster., Journal of the Warburg and Courtauld Institutes*, 1954, p.319.
H. Speed, *G. F. Watts' Law-Givers at Lincoln's Inn, Studio*, June, 1928, p.405.
W. H. Draper, *The Watts Frescoes at Lincoln's Inn, Burlington*, 1906, p.8.

WATTS AND WHITECHAPEL

Mrs. Barnett, *Canon Barnett, His Life, Work and Friends*, 1918.
W. T. Hill, *Octavia Hill*, 1956.
Magazine of Art, Vol. 3, 1880, p.210, *The Kyrle Society*.
E. Mackerness, *A Social History of English Music*, 1964.
Exhibition catalogue, *This is Whitechapel*, Whitechapel Art Gallery, London, 1973.

G. F. Watts.
Photograph attributed to Julia Margaret Cameron

APPENDIX II
The School of the Law Givers

Mr. G. F. Watts, who distinguished himself creditably in the first Government competition in connection with the rebuilding of the new Houses of Parliament, failing to receive patronage and encouragement in high quarters for the heroic in art, which he would aspire to, has come forward, gratuitously, we understand, to decorate the upper part of the north wall of Lincoln's-inn Hall with a grand fresco representing the early lawgivers from Moses down to Edward I., which self-imposed task he has just completed, and in a manner to redound much to his honour, and to offer encouragement, as we think, to those who would labour with him in the same lofty field. The dimensions of this work are about 45 feet wide by 40 feet high in the centre.

With regard to the technical execution, admitting some admirable drawing and a general breadth and treatment which indicates the presence of power and resource in the artist, we are compelled to state that in respect of colour the work is deficient – dull, crude, and obscure. Indeed, we fear we must admit that the pigments and vehicles necessary for fresco-painting, and which were employed in Italy by the great masters from the thirteenth to the fifteenth century, are as yet unknown to us; and, without them, any attempt at wall-painting, with the conditions attached to all wall-surfaces in this murky atmosphere of ours, must be comparatively failures. Fresco-painting, being seen at a distance, requires bright, pure, and, for the most part, simple colours, without graduated or mixed tints – the distance alone serving to soften and graduate

contrasting colours placed in the most abrupt contact. Above all, a good light should be vouchsafed to the picture, which in the case of the upper regions of the Gothic hall of Lincoln's-inn is a matter of simple impossibility, insomuch that the want of air which is complained of in the picture is, in our opinion, owing to the unfortunate circumstances under which it is seen. This disadvantage, we may add, is almost inseparable from Gothic architecture, which is unfavourable to the display of mural painting, except as employed for mere decorative purposes; and upon this ground we must deprecate the fashion, now so rife, of rushing into Gothic on all occasions of building a public edifice. Not to go to other examples, the grand defect in the new Houses of Parliament, and which is obvious throughout the building, with the exception perhaps of the actual chambers of the Legislature (which themselves are not Gothic), is want of light – a want which has all but extinguished many of the mural decorations in spite of an extravagant application of colour by the artist in a desperate effort to make his work seen.

In conclusion, let us say that, notwithstanding some shortcomings and many disadvantages under which it is viewed, Mr. Watts's fresco must be accepted with thanks, as one of the most important that has been attempted in our age or country – one highly creditable to his zeal and talent, and to his public spirit also, and of which the learned body whose edifice it graces may well be proud. (From the *Illustrated London News,* Feb. 4, 1860).

THE WORKS OF
MR. GEORGE F. WATTS, R.A.
WITH A
Complete Catalogue of his Pictures,
FOURTEEN DRAWINGS CONTRIBUTED BY HIMSELF,
AND OTHER ILLUSTRATIONS.

All rights reserved.] **Pall Mall Gazette "Extra."** No. 22.

EXPLANATORY.

BEFORE proceeding to give some account of the life-work of Mr. G. F. Watts, R.A., we are constrained to offer some explanation of the origin of this handbook, and to show how Mr. Watts, who has so courteously and generously assisted us in its preparation by contributing drawings of some of his principal pictures, touching them up with his own hand, and by giving us all the information in his power of which we stood in need, has been prevailed upon to thus apparently break through his constant and inflexible rule of declining in any way to come "before the public."

Mr. Watts has always been distinguished from all our other painters, with the exception perhaps of Mr. Ford Madox Brown, by his desire to carry on his work in private, neither seeking the applause of the public nor the eulogistic periods of the critic, and only so far emerging from his artistic retirement as the circumstances of life required. But the public, asserting its legitimate right, would not permit him to retain his works solely for the pleasure of those who chose, and who were able, to visit them in his own gallery at Little Holland House; and it claimed the privilege of seeing them how and where it liked. Recognizing, perhaps, with Dr. Johnson, that "modesty is a weakness if it suppresses virtue and hides it from the world," Mr. Watts has from time to time allowed himself to be persuaded to lend his pictures for exhibition *en bloc* at the Grosvenor Gallery, at Cardiff, at New York, and at Birmingham, on condition that all arrangements be made between the borrowers and

MR. G. F. WATTS, R.A.
(From a Special Sitting.)

his frame-maker, that he should not be called upon to act in any way, and that no personal reference should be made or introduced. The appreciation of the public of the cherished objects and aims of his lifetime cannot, of course, be indifferent to a man who has literally worked for the public far more than for himself; but his instinctive dread of appearing to thrust himself forward into their notice, as might naturally be expected, has had the effect of making him withdraw himself too much, and has caused him to regard all applications for information respecting his work and methods with a certain amount of suspicion or disquietude. When, after the reading by Mr. Horsley, R.A., of his now famous paper on the subject of "The Nude in Art," a representative of the *Pall Mall Gazette* called upon Mr. Watts, as the foremost painter of the nude in England, in order to ascertain his very pronounced views with reference to it, the latter incidentally remarked that he intended, as a "patriotic Englishman," leaving all, or nearly all, his works to the nation. This statement, which has indeed been made before, but never in so widely circulated a journal, nor in quite so public a manner, at once attracted a considerable amount of attention throughout the country, and the numerous expressions of satisfaction and curiosity, together with the simultaneous announcement on the part of the Corporation of Birmingham of the intention to inaugurate their new art galleries with loan collections of the works of Mr. Watts and Mr.

Burne-Jones, induced us to publish this description of his pictures. While not putting any difficulty in the way, Mr. Watts at first was very loth to offer any such assistance as might be construed into a desire for display, and it was only on our earnest representation that it was in the interests of the public that we desired to set forth the objects and achievements of his art, and that no reference of a purely personal character should be made—save in so far as was rendered necessary for the explanation of his works and the indication of the time of their execution, and so forth—that he concluded to help us ; and that he has done so to such good purpose that we are now enabled to set before our readers illustrations of some of his most famous pictures (most of them included in the Birmingham loan collection) drawn for us in chalk and touched by himself, and conveying in most instances, not only the composition of the works, but also that most difficult element to render, the spirit of them. And we take this opportunity of offering to him our sincere thanks for the trouble he has taken in the interest of the art-loving public, well knowing to what extent in acceding to our request he has gone against his own feelings in the matter.

MR. G. F. WATTS, R.A.

GEORGE FREDERICK WATTS, among all our living English masters the only absolutely self-taught one, was born in London in 1818. His strong instinctive love for the Fine Arts, which from the first pointed in the direction he has consistently followed ever since, early decided him to adopt them as his profession, and for this purpose he entered the so-called "school" of the Royal Academy to learn drawing. He left there, however, after an attendance of a few weeks, despairing to gain any instruction where nothing was taught—for the Royal Academy schools at that time were very different from what they are now—and, having an especial bent towards the plastic art, he entered the studio of the celebrated but unfortunate sculptor, William Behnes. Here it was his habit to watch the artist at work, but no other sort of instruction was imparted to him, as has erroneously been stated elsewhere. "I received no teaching," said Mr. Watts to the writer ; "I visited no painter's studio or *atelier.* Disappointed as to the Royal Academy, it became my habit to haunt the studio of Behnes, but I never studied under him in the ordinary acceptation of the term." The Elgin marbles—those supremely beautiful Parthenon fragments which Lord Elgin, at a cost of £35,000, lodged in the British Museum, amid the execrations of a violent minority—from the first delighted him, and the study of these perfect examples of the school of Phidias—some of them, in all probability, from the chisel of Phidias himself—is the origin of and may be traced in all Mr. Watts's greatest performances. Under the influence of these mighty works of art the youth worked on until the year 1837, when he contributed to the Royal Academy exhibition "A Wounded Heron" and two portraits of young ladies. These created a distinct impression, and he followed them up with pictures illustrative of scenes from Shakspeare and Boccaccio, and more portraits, all of which attracted still further notice and gave rise to hopes for his future success. For this he had not long to wait. In 1843, when the question of the decoration of the new Palace of Westminster was before the Royal Commission appointed for the purpose, nine prizes of £300, £200, and £100 were offered to the competitors. They were productive of no less than a hundred and forty cartoons,

ranging in length from ten to fifteen feet, which were opened and exhibited in Westminster Abbey in July of the same year. One of the first prizes was awarded to Mr. Watts's "Caractacus led in Triumph through the Streets of Rome," which ultimately, to the discredit of the Commissioners, was sold by auction for a nominal sum to a Bond-street dealer, who cut it up and sold it in separate pieces. Some of these are now in the possession of Sir Walter James. With the money thus acquired Mr. Watts was enabled to go to Rome, where he was hospitably received and entertained by the British Ambassador, in whose house he met many of the most celebrated men of the time, of some of whom he painted portraits. Here he would gaze at the works of the Venetian school, whose exquisite colour naturally awakened his enthusiastic admiration ; but, contrary to the usual practice, and with curious independence of spirit, he refrained from making any copies or studies, properly so called ; feeling, no doubt, with Eupompus of Sicyon, that Nature and not an artist should be his master. In Italy he spent four years, and when he returned to England he brought with him several works painted more or less under the influence of the great Venetian masters, among which were the colossal pictures "Echo" and "King Alfred inciting the Saxons to prevent the Landing of the Danes." The latter he sent in to a second competition at Westminster, and he again won a first prize (this time of £500), and he was further entrusted with a commission for the picture "St. George overcomes the Dragon," since gravely described, with official acumen, as "St. George *welcomes* the Dragon." This work, which was begun in 1848, was not completed until 1853, and it may now be seen in the Upper Waiting Hall, beside the Central Hall of the Palace.

APPENDIX IV

George Frederick Watts

A somewhat unusual note of coolness and caution has tinged most of the notices of Watts's life and work that have hitherto appeared. We are so accustomed to the unstinted praise of dead mediocrities that this coolness almost implies that as a painter Mr. Watts, in spite of the loftiness of his aims, was almost less than a mediocrity. This tendency may in part be due to a reaction from such excessive praise, and in part to want of perspective, although as so much of Watts's painting belongs to an earlier generation than ours there ought to be little difficulty in making a fair estimate of his rank.

We are inclined to think that custom has much to do with this hesitancy. Mr. Watts was lavish both in painting pictures and in presenting them to the public, so that his departure is the departure of a personality almost too familiar for impartial admiration. His reputation, for the moment, thus suffers in comparison with that of an artist like Whistler, whose genius was always surrounded with a certain glamour of remoteness.

It is generally recognized that Watts stood alone in embodying the larger sentiments of our time in a dignified and splendid form, a form which use, as in the case of Fitzgerald's Omar Khayyam, has made for the moment almost too easy of approach. The criticism is hardly fair, for we accept unchallenged a similar facility in the Bible stories told by Rembrandt and Michelangelo.

Then, having hesitated over a simplicity which is in reality the result of supreme synthetic power, we grow still more doubtful over Watts's technique. We admit the variety of his achievement in portraiture and landscape and figure painting, as well as the grandeur of his design, his unerring pictorial sense, and the beauty-force and emphasis of his colour; but one and all we appear to think that he could not paint.

Watts's open avowal of a didactic aim may have had something to do with this: may not the rest be the result of a contemporary fashion? The modern ideal of technique is based upon that part of the achievement of Velazquez which Mr. Sargent expounds so brilliantly. This obvious directness of brushwork is a wonderful thing, but the subtle power and splendour of a Titian has behind it a far greater reserve of knowledge and beauty. May not the apparent hesitation in Mr. Watts's work be due to the need of suggesting more than the crisp presentment of a momentary aspect can suggest, just as the summary modelling of his forms is due to the necessity of subordinating unessential facts to general breadth of effect? His peculiar use of pigment in the same way was the result of a deliberate purpose to combine richness and luminosity with that permanent freshness which is best secured by working without a liquid medium, and by the trusting to time to smooth and blend any roughness of surface or sharpness of contrast. For these reasons we think that the future may accord to Watts as an executant almost the high place which it must accord to him as a creative designer and as a colourist; a place by the side of Rubens and Titian, and so little short of the summit of human achievement in the arts that it is perhaps natural we should hesitate to recognize its loftiness at once.

Obituary from: *The Burlington Magazine,* Vol. 5, 1904, p. 452.

Mr and Mrs Watts in the studio, 6 Melbury Road

No. 10: Peasants of the Campagna During The Vintage. *Photograph: A. C. Cooper Ltd*

No. 13: Under a Dry Arch. *Photograph: A. C. Cooper Ltd*

No. 25: The Denunication of Cain
Photograph: John Donat

No.26: Paolo and Francesca. *Photograph: John Donat*

No. 31: The Carrara Mountains

No. 41: The Sphynx. *Photograph: John Donat*

No. 47: Love and Life